Praise for *Missional Communities*

"Once again, Reggie McNeal proclaims what too few have intuited: that God's Spirit is blowing in a new direction like a hurricane headwind. It is a gale force that we can lean against, be rolled by, or ride to new heights. Thank God, we have Reggie to show us how the church can once more 'mount up with wings as eagles.'"

—Charles Anderson, directing pastor,
University United Methodist Church, San Antonio, TX

"Every uncharted territory requires a guide that has seen the other side of the mountain. In *Missional Communities* Reggie serves as that guide who introduces you to the people, practices, and scorecard of this fresh growth plate of the kingdom."

—Eric Swanson, coauthor,
The Externally Focused Quest and *To Transform a City*

"Reggie is an iconoclast. His ideas and vision break open our sense of what it means to 'be' and 'do' church. If you love God and believe in the future of the church you will read this book."

—Rev. Chip Edens, rector,
Christ Church, Charlotte, NC

"Once again, Reggie McNeal has been reading my mind! He has given voice to those of us who dream of a church that is not just a conspiracy of strangers but a redemptive community on a mission for God. For those who dare to make the journey this book provides some invaluable navigational charts for how to get there."

—Gary Brandenburg, lead pastor,
Fellowship Bible Church Dallas, Dallas, TX

"Classic Reggie McNeal! An in-your-face prophetic wake-up call that congregational ministry business as usual is not going to get the job done in days ahead. But he gives us hope that we can make the change as he reports on how post-congregational ministry is being effective."

—Buford Lipscomb, senior pastor,
Liberty Church, Pensacola, FL

"Our staff team at Christ Fellowship has been deeply impacted by the challenges and thinking of Reggie McNeal. He has served us by helping us think beyond ourselves, reminding us that true community results in mission and continually bringing us back to the glorious mission of Jesus."

—Eric Geiger, Christ Fellowship,
Miami, FL

MISSIONAL
COMMUNITIES

Missional Communities

The Rise of the Post-Congregational Church

Reggie McNeal

Foreword by Hugh Halter

A Leadership Network Publication

JOSSEY-BASS
A Wiley Imprint
www.josseybass.com

Published by Jossey-Bass
A Wiley Imprint
989 Market Street, San Francisco, CA 94103-1741—www.josseybass.com

Readers should be aware that Internet websites offered as citations and/or sources for further information may have changed or disappeared between the time this was written and when it is read.

Jossey-Bass books and products are available through most bookstores. To contact Jossey-Bass directly call our Customer Care Department within the U.S. at 800-956-7739, outside the U.S. at 317-572-3986, or fax 317-572-4002.

Jossey-Bass also publishes its books in a variety of electronic formats. Some content that appears in print may not be available in electronic books.

Library of Congress Cataloging-in-Publication Data
McNeal, Reggie.
  Missional communities : the rise of the post-congregational church / Reggie McNeal.—1st ed.
     p. cm.— (Jossey-Bass leadership network series ; 55)
  Includes index.
  ISBN 978-0-470-63345-8 (hardback); 978-1-118-10758-4 (ebk); 978-1-118-10759-1 (ebk); 978-1-118-10760-7 (ebk)
1. Church development, New. 2. Church. 3. Church renewal. 4. Postmodernism—Religious aspects—Christianity. 5. Christianity—Forecasting. I. Title.
  BV652.24.M38 2011
  266—dc23
                                                                 2011021311

Printed in the United States of America
FIRST EDITION
HB Printing   10 9 8 7 6 5 4 3 2 1

LEADERSHIP NETWORK TITLES

133607

Church Unique: How Missional Leaders Cast Vision, Capture Culture, and Create Movement, Will Mancini

A New Kind of Christian: A Tale of Two Friends on a Spiritual Journey, Brian D. McLaren

The Story We Find Ourselves In: Further Adventures of a New Kind of Christian, Brian D. McLaren

Missional Communities: The Rise of the Post-Congregational Church, Reggie McNeal

Missional Renaissance: Changing the Scorecard for the Church, Reggie McNeal

Practicing Greatness: 7 Disciplines of Extraordinary Spiritual Leaders, Reggie McNeal

The Present Future: Six Tough Questions for the Church, Reggie McNeal

A Work of Heart: Understanding How God Shapes Spiritual Leaders, Reggie McNeal

The Millennium Matrix: Reclaiming the Past, Reframing the Future of the Church, M. Rex Miller

Your Church in Rhythm: The Forgotten Dimensions of Seasons and Cycles, Bruce B. Miller

Shaped by God's Heart: The Passion and Practices of Missional Churches, Milfred Minatrea

The Missional Leader: Equipping Your Church to Reach a Changing World, Alan J. Roxburgh and Fred Romanuk

Missional Map-Making: Skills for Leading in Times of Transition, Alan J. Roxburgh

Relational Intelligence: How Leaders Can Expand Their Influence Through a New Way of Being Smart, Steve Saccone

Viral Churches: Helping Church Planters Become Movement Makers, Ed Stetzer and Warren Bird

The Externally Focused Quest: Becoming the Best Church for the Community, Eric Swanson and Rick Rusaw

The Ascent of a Leader: How Ordinary Relationships Develop Extraordinary Character and Influence, Bill Thrall, Bruce McNicol, and Ken McElrath

Beyond Megachurch Myths: What We Can Learn from America's Largest Churches, Scott Thumma and Dave Travis

The Other 80 Percent: Turning Your Church's Spectators into Active Participants, Scott Thumma and Warren Bird

The Elephant in the Boardroom: Speaking the Unspoken About Pastoral Transitions, Carolyn Weese and J. Russell Crabtree

CONTENTS

To all the pioneers in the missional
community movement

ABOUT THE JOSSEY-BASS LEADERSHIP NETWORK SERIES

Leadership Network's mission is to accelerate the impact of OneHundredX leaders. These high-capacity leaders are like the hundredfold crop that comes from seed planted in good soil as Jesus described in Matthew 13:8.

Leadership Network . . .

- Explores the "what's next?" of what could be
- Creates "aha!" environments for collaborative discovery
- Works with exceptional "positive deviants"
- Invests in the success of others through generous relationships
- Pursues big impact through measurable kingdom results
- Strives to model Jesus through all we do

Believing that meaningful conversations and strategic connections can change the world, we seek to help leaders navigate the future by exploring new ideas and finding application for each unique context. Through collaborative meetings and processes, leaders map future possibilities and challenge one another to action that accelerates fruitfulness and effectiveness. Leadership Network shares the learnings and inspiration with others through our books, concept papers, research reports, e-newsletters, podcasts, videos, and online experiences. This in turn generates a ripple effect of new conversations and further influence.

In 1996 Leadership Network established a partnership with Jossey-Bass, a Wiley Imprint, to develop a series of creative books that provide thought leadership to innovators in church ministry. Leadership Network Publications present thoroughly researched and innovative concepts from leading thinkers, practitioners, and pioneering churches.

Leadership Network is a division of OneHundredX, a global ministry with initiatives around the world.

To learn more about Leadership Network, go to www .leadnet.org

To learn more about OneHundredX, go to www.100x.org

FOREWORD

Exhausted, jaded, and vowing never to return to leading another consumeristic church expression, my family and two other families moved to Denver to start a missions community ... a missional community. As we spent 90 percent of our time and every Sunday with lost people, we stumbled into a story that not only surprised us but also forced us to rethink everything. Eventually another church just happened without our trying to start one!

At first it wasn't about reaching the lost. It was about recovering our own hearts. We wanted to find rhythms of life that were fun, made sense, and were easy to invite others into. As we tried to make the Kingdom tangible to ourselves, we found many disoriented saints and sinners who found our home their home, who followed us in mission, and who found the God we were reorienting our lives around.

At the time, we didn't have any language for it. We had not developed any concepts for reproducing it and we were sure we were the only crazy people sniffing a new fragrance of Kingdom church. All we knew was that it felt right and we were grateful that God had wooed us into his original design.

Imagine what it would be like if our world were like the rest of the world. Maybe like communist China where the largest Christian movement in history is still happening under our noses without all the bells and whistles of paid staff or church buildings. Maybe like postearthquake Japan, where entire churches were leveled and where God's people have to rearrange everything just to stay together. Be it financial disasters, constant war, or a big hole in the ocean floor leaking thousands of gallons of oil into the Gulf, someday soon, people won't just load up the family in a minivan for a twenty-minute drive across town to hear the preacher encourage them for the week. Someday soon, people are going to be desperate for a few friends in their own neighborhood to huddle around scripture, mission, and life.

Missional community is exactly what would happen if we *had* to be real Christians. And we may be getting there sooner than we think.

Regardless of the form of church in which you now participate, Reggie McNeal is helping all of us get ahead of a conversation God is now having with the whole church. No, this book isn't about organic church or house church or telling you to go small. This book is about going *big* by returning to our base nature, our primal function, and the most substantive substructure of New Testament church ... the missional community.

Unlike most prophets who frustrate open-hearted leaders with concepts and ecclesial configurations that leave you without any tangible way to proceed, Reggie pulls the curtains back and flings open practitioner-based windows of real people in real life cities and suburbs. As he does so, you'll feel the fresh air of hope and you'll have more of a sense of where and how to go with these ideas.

Missional community is not a threat to traditional churches or theology unless you're only in it for yourself, unless you want to remain mired in the mud of consumer church, or unless you wish to continue creating disciples of the world instead of disciples of Jesus. This book is for

Kingdom leaders who want to be a part of the systemic transformation of the church!

Although you'll be pushed, Reggie will inspire you to throw your hat into the ring with thousands who courageously experiment, improve, and add their story to the Kingdom mosaic God is artistically arranging.

Hugh Halter

ACKNOWLEDGMENTS

Every book published represents a collaborative effort to differing degrees. In this case, with the heart of the book being a collection of stories, I am indebted to a bunch of people whose work I chronicle. Mike Breen of 3D Ministries, Rich Robinson of St. Thomas Philadelphia and Tom Finnemore of St. Thomas Crookes made the telling of the St. Thomas Sheffield experience possible. Sune Andersen brought me up to speed on the developments in Aarhus. Caesar Kalinowski served as host and narrator for my trip to experience Soma Communities. Justin Christopher was my field guide at the University of Texas at Austin, putting together my tour there and securing notes from student leaders Jenny Dietz, Peter Schulte, Raul Garcia, and Rachel Alvarez. My friend Alan Hirsch contributed the introduction and background for Future Travelers. Michael "Stew" Stewart and Todd Engstrom provided commentary for the Austin Stone missional community journey. Eric Metcalf pulled together the Community Christian team—including Dave Ferguson, Pat Masek, Carter Moss, Kim Hammond, and Kirsten Strand. Jim Herrington and Steve Capper brought me up to speed with their work at Mission Houston. Hugh Halter set the whole book up with a wonderful foreword. The eager and generous response of these leaders reflects the passion that characterizes the missional communities movement.

Of course, getting stories into print requires a publisher. The crack team of Sheryl Fullerton (my editor now on our third book together), Alison Knowles, and Joanne Clapp Fullagar at Jossey-Bass make this part easy (well—at least for me!).

The publishing team at Leadership Network are not just colleagues but friends. Mark Sweeney (thanks for believing), Greg Ligon, and Stephanie Plagens form an awesome trinity of talent and strategy for our multiple publishing series.

The people we do life with, our missional community, read each chapter and gave thoughtful feedback. I owe them much more than editorial appreciation. They are an ongoing source of joy and encouragement.

Finally, no author has a more raving fan than I do. Cathy, you keep me going in every way.

INTRODUCTION

Toward the end of *Missional Renaissance*, published by Jossey-Bass in 2009, I made the following assertion: "I have argued that we must expand the bandwidth of what forms church should take, including many noninstitutional expressions.... [F]orms of missional communities are developing and will have their own appeal. Instead of excoriating these developments, why not champion them?" Although I was confident in my prediction I have been caught off guard by how quickly the development of this alternative church form is taking off. Church as missional community has arrived. And it is here to stay.

In retrospect I should not be surprised. Almost a decade ago, in *The Present Future*, I talked about the emergence of post-congregationalist Christians as a significant and growing phenomenon affecting church attendance. At that time, I quoted David Barrett, author of the *World Christian Encyclopedia*, who estimated there are about 112 million "churchless Christians" worldwide, about 5 percent of all adherents, but he projects that number will double in the next twenty years! These post-congregational Christians are people who, for a variety of reasons, choose to pursue their spiritual journey outside the routines and rhythms of the congregational model of church that has dominated the church landscape for centuries. This development, coupled with the growing eclectic street spirituality in our culture, has created ripe conditions to produce and to nurture a new life form. It is a concept of church that intersects people in the middle of life—in their homes, their workplaces, their leisure pursuits, and their passions to help others.

Missional communities are not clergy dependent; they have a rhythm that is unique to them and express themselves in ways that reflect the life in their center. They grow in habitats beyond the reach of the institutional church, in environments that will not sustain the traditional practices of church. Missional communities are not focused on their corporate vision. They don't implore their members for support. They have no life beyond the life of the people who constitute the community.

Typically missional communities have no buildings to maintain and, in many cases, no clergy to support. Their scorecard is simple—are people of the community experiencing the abundant life Jesus promised and are they sharing it with others? Loving God and loving their neighbor, loving God by loving their neighbor—these are the rails that the missional community runs on.

The rhythms of missional communities differ from the artificial every-seven-days life and business cycle of the congregational and programmatic modality of church. The "whens" and "whats" of the community are established by the lifestyles and life interests of the people who comprise the community, not the other way around. There is no sense of necessity that everything must be done every week. A more organic view prevails—one of seasons, not clocks.

The disciplines of missional communities can also differ sharply from traditional church practice. The institutional church, with its goal of participation, helps people develop the disciplines of attendance and giving and serving the church. Privatized disciplines such as prayer, fasting, and scripture reading are encouraged but not necessary to sustain the program-based congregation. Missional communities, however, have maturation as their end game—developing people who are increasingly identifiable as followers of Jesus. Communal practice and personal formation are intertwined because each person expresses the life of the community incarnated in him or her. Disciplines of generosity, service, transparency, compassion, and grace—these are the necessary commitments to build and to sustain community.

Only a distorted or incomplete understanding of what missional community is would cause someone to determine that church in this form is less demanding and more self-centered than traditional church. In fact, just the opposite can be argued. The consumerist model of program church typically requires only that its members support it. And, as long as the program delivers what they want and expect, people will. In addition, being a church member doesn't require getting along with or having to like other members. However, being community carries with it the prerequisite of dealing with the others in community, working through differences. Being in community requires a commitment for a person to journey beyond self.

Missional community is a different expression of church than its congregational cousin. It differs in its rhythm, celebrations, activities, and scorecard. It is not for everyone, nor is it the replacement of centuries of church practice. But it is a growing phenomenon and these pages are dedicated to telling part of its story.

To help you gain a feel for what I am talking about I have chosen a range of missional community expressions and practices. Each chapter will detail one way some people are practicing missional community. The settings range from

Europe to North America, from suburb to city to college campus, from neighborhood to workplace. The idea is not just to inform you but to excite your imagination. Some of you who are reading this want to explore this way of being church for yourself, your family, and your friends. This should help you get started, maybe even to figure out a distinctive way of doing missional community by combining various elements of the approaches presented in this book. Others of you are leaders of churches who are gaining a greater sense of call to be a missional strategist, not just an institutional manager. You might discover in these pages a way forward to exponentially increase your "reach" in your city or town while carrying on your traditional churching practices.

Some of you are reading to find out what's wrong with this, searching for data to bolster your arguments aimed at protecting and defending the traditional church against this development. I hope you will read with an open mind. Don't confuse your psychological needs—for control, order, and security—with theology. The way of being church in the world began to shift in the book of Acts and carries on into today. Just because you can't find your way by adopting this way does not mean others who do aren't following The Way.

Before we begin our visits to various missional communities, it will help to know what we are looking at and what we are looking for. That's a good place to begin.

MISSIONAL COMMUNITIES

1

"LET THERE BE ... MISSIONAL COMMUNITIES"

The e-mails come every week or so. They usually begin with something like: "I feel called to start a church but I don't want to replicate the existing model." Maybe they are a bit more specific: "The church plant I have in mind doesn't center on a worship service; it functions more like a network of people engaged in serving the community." Often the e-mailers are not clergy; they are frustrated church members. They say something like, "I am just not happy any more being a religious consumer—I want to get outside the walls of the church." Or, "I am tired of just doing church over and over; shouldn't we be paying more attention to what we do with the rest of our week?" Then typically the senders raise a question: "Do you know of anyone else thinking like this?"

Yes, I do. Thousands, actually. And they are doing something about it.

We are witnessing the rise of a new life form in the taxonomy of the North American church. Though it contains the DNA of the movement that Jesus founded, its expression is different from the institutional church that has developed over the centuries. It is church in a new way for a new day—our day—a period that can be described as the post-congregational era of Christianity. This new church life form is the missional community.

There you have it! This is the essence of the book's message. Rather than making you wait to get the point—here it is, up-front. Perhaps now that you know, you'd rather not read any further—this phenomenon doesn't interest you. But if you want to know more, perhaps even explore your own possible involvement, by all means read on.

The heart of this book is the telling of stories about some of the various approaches to these new missional communities. Each story is different, illustrating a fresh chapter in God's work in and through the church. By showing you some early iterations of missional communities, my hope is that your own imagination will be excited, possibly to the point of your trying your own hand at it!

In many ways the rise of missional communities takes the church back to its early days, when it was a movement, before it became church-as-we-know-it. Before it became church as congregation.

Church as Congregation

For most of Christian history congregations have served as gathering places where geographically approximate adherents could practice their faith. It was not always this way.

For most of its first three centuries Christianity was mainly a street movement, a marketplace phenomenon that spread through slave populations and social guilds of free laborers. Gatherings of adherents took place primarily in homes and some suitable public places, convening primarily for fellowship, teaching, and worship. However, the gatherings were not the point or focus of Jesus-follower spirituality. Christianity was primarily a practice, a way of life.

Love of God and love of neighbor meant adopting a life of sacrificial service that distinguished followers of Jesus as a counter-cultural force, differentiated from those around them by the character of their lives. Early believers rescued babies (especially girls) abandoned by Roman households. They stayed behind to tend to the sick people when plagues drove the population out of the cities. In other words, Jesus followers demonstrated allegiance to Jesus primarily when they were away from their gatherings, engaged in lives that typically and routinely intersected with and included non-Jesus followers. The church represented a lifestyle that was radically different from its cultural surroundings but radically committed to the well-being of the people in the culture.

Along the way, though, this orientation changed. The church movement became domesticated. The imperial edict by Constantine is usually blamed but a shift was already under way with the rise of a clergy class. These two forces—the need to create a state religion and a clergy eager to comply—combined to centralize and institutionalize the Christian movement. The church congregationalized. This move profoundly altered its way of being in the world.

The idea of adherents gathering together as the central practice of the faith gained ascendancy when the church settled down into a religion dominated by clergy. Church as congregation developed the expectation that people would demonstrate their devotion to the faith by participating in congregational activity, which centrally involved the worship service. Rather than a lifestyle of counter-cultural sacrificial love of neighbor, adherence to "the faith" became centered on assenting to a set of doctrinal beliefs. Christianity became defined as a set of theological propositions rather than a way of life.

The ensuing schism between belief and practice promoted a sacred-secular dichotomy that greatly influenced the nature of congregational life as something distinct from the rest of life. Church became a "sacred place" where specific religious acts were performed. The congregation served as home base for Jesus followers, a sort of refuge, effectively pulling the church off the streets. Loyalty to Christ was measured by one's participation in congregational activity. In exchange for this support the church provided religious goods and services to its "members." The "member culture" would eventually give rise to a culture of competition, as congregations vied for the affection and financial support of existing and potential customers.

The most enduring legacy of the congregational church is its worldview. Church as congregation became something other than the people who were its constituency. The church became an "it." It stood outside people. This notion is in contradiction to the New Testament understanding of church as a "who." Biblical teaching on the church sees the church as the ongoing incarnation of Jesus in the world, an organic life form vitally connected to him, even married to him, depending on the metaphor chosen by the writer. Church as an "it" followed the inevitable path that all institutions travel. Institutional goals eventually became separated from and supplanted spiritual mission. The clergy, who initially served as spiritual leaders because they were *spiritual* leaders, over centuries became increasingly captured by organizational concerns at best or political agendas in the worst cases.

Although the Reformation adjusted some of the theological categories, it did little to alter the notion of church as a congregational expression. In fact, Reformation ecclesiology remained centered on the congregation. Church vocations still referred to clergy roles. Orders and practices guided and focused on what the church did in its corporate gatherings, worship, and activities. In many denominations the idea of church itself became inextricably tied to the proper administration and functioning of gatherings, worship, and activities, especially if it was a way of distinguishing one denominational tribe from another.

The post-Reformation modern era did not move to alter the congregational understanding of church. Though several developments affected its practices, nothing challenged the ruling paradigm of church as congregation. Twentieth-century developments in transportation and the corresponding infrastructure such as freeways allowed people to travel greater distances more quickly with relative ease. People could choose among congregations to select their spiritual "home." This, in turn, fueled congregational competition, giving rise to the customer-service orientation of the contemporary program church (and spawned a church growth industry that promoted the idea of building even bigger and better "churches"—meaning congregational organizations). The assumption was that community and individual transformation would result from having great congregations with well-trained clergy and lots of programs.

The rise of the megachurch in the second half of the twentieth century paralleled what was going on in the retail world as the center of gravity shifted from the "mom-and-pop parish" to the large "big box retail centers." These megachurches have maintained their core sense of identity as a congregation—that is, for those who attend, church is something outside of me that I belong to, that I attend or "go to," an institution that I support.

This sweeping and admittedly broad-brush treatment of church development over the centuries might sound as if church as congregation is and was bad. I do not mean to imply or even to suggest this. To the contrary, many congregations do a lot of good. Some pack hundreds of backpacks of food every week to send home with school children who are food insecure. Others conduct mentoring and tutoring programs for underperforming students. Some churches are building wells in overseas villages so people can have access to clean water while at the same time creating microeconomic development opportunities for the villagers. Still others work to liberate women and children from sex trafficking and slavery. Certainly without congregational effort, the clean-up efforts after Hurricane Katrina would have been far less extensive and effective. In fact, the faith community saved the day for many—and is still working to rebuild that part of our country. Disaster relief abroad as well would be much diminished without the altruism expressed through American congregations. Added to all this is the spiritual teaching and nurturing of millions of Americans each week! All of this should be honored and celebrated.

Nor do I mean to seem to be predicting the end of the congregational expression of Christianity. Millions are served in their spiritual journeys through its efforts and millions more are helped to enjoy a better life through its ministry. The congregation is here to stay!

I am simply trying to point out that this one view of church has been so predominant in Western culture that it has made it seem as if it is the only legitimate expression. Anything that takes place outside of "church as congregation" has seemed suspicious to some. Even terms like *para-church*—a word that makes no sense biblically (one is either in the church or not)—is an organizational term invented to affirm the supremacy of church as congregation. It has taken years for the house church movement to gain respect, even though it was the predominant form of church expression in the first three centuries of the Christian movement and is a potent life form in countries where the church is growing virally.

What I am after here is opening up the discussion of missional communities so that we can begin to see that God is up to something new. I am suggesting that we expand the bandwidth of how we think church can express itself in our culture.

We need to or else we are in real trouble.

Even with the rise of megacongregations, decades of emphasis on church growth, and large infusions of money and people resources, the congregational approach to "doing church" has entered its declining period. Church attendance is holding up as well as it is only because Americans are living longer. Even so, participation is slipping. The prognostication is not good. A variety of indicators all point to the same conclusion: we have entered an era that is ripe for and needs a post-congregational church.

The Post-Congregational Era

For millions of Americans, the congregational form of church expression does not work for them. They either cannot or will not convert to the church culture. Many of them cannot match its participation rhythms because of their employment. They work in the hospitality industry, in health care, or in some capacity in which they serve as first responders (like police, fire protection), in public utilities, or in a host of entertainment industry options. Simply put, these people don't have the weekend off from work to "go to church." Millions more have lifestyles that don't accommodate church attendance or engagement. Weekends might be spent visiting children of ex-marriages or be filled with leisure pursuits or kids' sports leagues.

The numbers tell the story. The fastest growing religious affiliation in the country is the "non-affiliated"—a category that has doubled in the past fifteen years! This designation reflects a rejection not just of Christianity but every organized religion (Hinduism, Buddhism, Wicca, and so on). One out of six Americans (16 percent) says he or she doesn't wish to be identified with any existing group. Underneath that number are two startling findings: the rate of nonaffiliation is 20 percent of men and a whopping 25 percent of young adults ages eighteen to twenty-nine! These "nones" are not antispiritual. Half of them believe in God and the Bible. It's just that they are not turning to institutional, traditional church as part of their spiritual journey. They are not alone. More than one in five Americans who say they are absolutely sure about believing in God virtually never attend church, according to the research of Robert Putnam published in his recent book *American Grace* (Simon and Schuster, 2010, p. 473). This does not portend well for the future of the congregational church expression.

Just in case you are wondering if these diminished numbers could be turned around with aggressive marketing and outreach, don't hold your breath or call a committee meeting. The number of people who say they would attend a church if invited has trended downward dramatically over the past four decades. Gallup polling confirms this in reporting a near-record high in the percentage of people who say that religion is losing its influence in America.

These developments have come about while we have been building the best churches we have ever had—complete with waterfalls, executive chefs, and weekly productions rivaling anything Broadway can produce. The American church now gobbles up over $100 billion per year for all causes, including media outlets, schools, real estate development, and church programming—with increasingly less return on investment! The nonchurched aren't comin'—no matter what we do!

We would be wrong to read this allergic response to church as an indication of a decline in spirituality in our country. Americans remain incredibly intrigued by all things spiritual. After decades and even centuries of secular humanistic philosophical arguments, Americans still believe in God. Atheism and agnosticism capture a fraction of the population (8 percent). In fact, spirituality is in vogue, whether on the Oprah cable network, the movies, the speeches of politicians, or the spirituality sections of bookstores. It's just that people aren't seeing church as the way they want to pursue their spiritual journey.

We are whipped if we consider church as congregation as the only true expression of church. But it's not. We have options.

Taking a Page from Our Past ... for the Future

We can look to the earliest days of the Christian movement to find those options. At that time, the popularity of the gospel was drawing in a huge number of non-Jewish people. Gentiles eagerly responded to the invitation of the early Jesus followers to join them in the new faith but that trend didn't thrill everyone. Some began to insist that Gentiles should become Jews first in order to receive the gospel. After considerable deliberations (the Acts 15 conference) the church declared this step to be unnecessary. New spiritual realities in the first century successfully broke down old religious categories and approaches. With this single decision the church secured its future—avoiding becoming a sect of Judaism and instead launching a global missionary movement. Bottom line: early church leaders refused to force people to become like them in order to become Jesus followers.

The corresponding issue for the church in North America today is whether or not we are going to insist that people first become church people in order to experience the gospel of Jesus. If we do we will seal our fate as an institution that will continue to diminish as fewer and fewer people fit our profile. We will miss the spiritual revival that is under way. And we will miss the heartbeat of a missional God who is always seeking us no matter where we try to hide—whether in urban centers, suburban malls, or church pews.

Not insisting that people become like us in order to follow Jesus does not mean we have to abandon our own personal spiritual preferences and practices. In fact, as you will see, many people participating in missional communities are retaining their congregational affiliation. A perspective informed by the first-century church wisdom simply acknowledges that God encounters others in ways that are different from our own experience. In our time that "different" way increasingly appears to be a missional community setting. In the stories that follow you will learn that some of this new expression of church is even being sponsored by existing congregational leaders who see that church as congregation *and* church as missional community both fit into their strategy for sharing the gospel.

The good news is that many people who are not intrigued to become part of the church culture are nevertheless wide open to spiritual engagement. People who would never attend a church service will bring their entire families to help feed the homeless or serve meals to disaster victims—and have spiritual conversation with others while doing it. And some who would never consider joining a congregation will enthusiastically participate in a group setting in a neighbor's home where Bible study, prayer, and life debriefing take place.

The further good news is that this is where Jesus is hanging out anyway. The church culture I grew up in challenged me to "lead lost people to Jesus." The assumption was that Jesus's preferred environment was the church ("where two or three are gathered"), and the world was a godless and hostile environment that we were to take Jesus into. I now understand that "lost people will lead *me* to Jesus." After all, Jesus said, "The Son of Man came to seek and to save the lost" (Luke 19:10). This means that Jesus is already in the world, inviting church people out to play! We run into Jesus in homeless shelters, battered women's homes, high-rise offices, hospital waiting rooms, AIDS clinics—wherever people need him, Jesus makes a point of being there.

And what am I supposed to do when I connect people with Jesus? The church as congregation culture taught me to "reach" people for Christ, meaning "turn them into church people." The path to discipleship led to the church door. Their adopting a congregational life rhythm and lifestyle was the proof we sought that life transformation had occurred. The problem today is that people don't want to be "reached" by the church and turned into church people. They have had friends "reached" and it's like they have been abducted by aliens. They can't find their friends anymore—they are now living in the mother ship. Sadly, church as congregation has become very good at socializing its people away from the very mission field where God placed them.

This reality hit home to me on a recent airplane flight. I wasn't eavesdropping. It's just that in a small regional jet, if the people seated behind you decide to carry on a conversation, then you are smack dab in the middle of it. Their physical proximity makes it impossible to avoid hearing every word they say. On the flight I sat in front of two guys who chatted the entire trip, mostly about playing golf and their travels. Both were headed home. Just as we were landing the younger of the two identified himself as a staff member of a local congregation and invited his seat mate to church. "We've got a lot of good things going on," he said proudly. The other passenger politely made it plain he was not interested. "I play golf every Sunday," he said. "Well," the church staffer replied, "if you ever get rained out, we'd love to have you." That was it. No mention of God. No spiritual inquiry. No connection. The conversation ended.

Last week I spoke at a conference where a denominational executive took some time to tell the attendees about his latest "witnessing" opportunity. It involved the neurosurgeon he was newly seeing for a health issue that had cropped up. When the doctor inquired about the executive's occupation, he said he was a minister. The doctor, a Hindu, then initiated a conversation inquiring about the patient's basis for believing in Jesus. The minister brought him a book on apologetics on his next visit. "I don't have time to read that," the doctor said. "Why don't you tell me what's in it?" At this point the clergy person invited the physician to church! The doctor replied, "I'd rather have tea and talk with you." On revealing that request from his doctor, the platform speaker said, "Pray for me as I continue to 'witness' to my doctor." My response was to urge him to have tea. "Don't talk *church*. This guy is looking for God," I said. He looked bewildered at my suggestion, if not a little offended.

These two episodes reveal the major limitations of church as congregation and why alternative church life forms are needed. We need to reverse the trend of replacing gospel messages with church marketing. Because the congregational church model relies on attracting new members to sustain its business model, this dynamic has been reinforced for centuries. But we are seeing the end of the success of this model. A declining percentage of the population relegates their spiritual quest to a prescribed set of religious activities conducted at a specific place and time. More and more people are either unable or unwilling to alter their life rhythms to match congregational rhythms and expectations in order to pursue their spiritual journeys.

A post-congregational culture requires a strategy of engaging people right where they already live, work, play, go to school, and pursue their hobbies and passions. It's incarnational. It lets them live more intentionally, learning to love God and their neighbors more, making a contribution to their community, all with people they know and are known by. This is the recipe for a new church life form—missional communities.

2

THE MISSIONAL CHURCH CONVERSATION

For 1,700 years the church has focused primarily on its "gathered" mode of being. Buildings have been constructed to house gathered congregations. Clergy have developed liturgy for worship service gatherings. Worship leaders have rehearsed choirs, praise teams, bands, orchestras, and drama groups to lead the gatherings. Pastors have produced sermons to deliver to the assembled church. Church theology has been written largely with the gathered, corporate church in mind—from the discussion of calling and giftedness to the description of how the church conducts its various functions. Training for church leaders has focused on equipping them to guide the gathered church in its worship, evangelism and outreach, teaching and discipleship, pastoral care, fellowship, and missions programs. If all these congregation-centric activities and programs went well, we knew we were successful. Our metrics celebrated that success.

Although we acknowledged that the church also had a "scattered" dimension, that realm of church life received very little attention over the centuries and served mainly to designate the periods between the gatherings. "Real" church, everyone knew, happened when the church came together as congregation. "Scattered" church, the time between gatherings, was considered the separate, private domain of church members engaged in their life pursuits and occupations. The hope was that what happened at church influenced these other life compartments but "church" was reserved for congregation-specific activities. Consequently, the dispersed church failed to have the clarity of purpose that church as congregation enjoyed.

What we have not had for all these centuries is robust attention to the "sent" aspect of church. The "sent" church implies a church on mission, largely played out away from church gatherings. "Sent" people maintain the purpose of the church when scattered and are not just hanging around waiting for the next church gathering to attend to and live out their spiritual development.

It seems that God is initiating a new conversation with the church about this dimension of being sent. This dialog is certainly not accidental. Because people increasingly aren't coming to the traditional church as congregation for their spiritual guidance and experience, the impetus for going out to them has reemerged. The missional conversation has created a new discussion about the role of the church *in the world*. The theme focuses on the "sentness" of the church—the commission of the church as being sent to engage the world with the gospel. This emphasis is serving as a corrective to a truncated truth: that the church is the "called out" (the Greek *ekklesia*) people of God. Although this is true, it is not the whole truth. The complete truth is that we have been "called out" to be "sent back."

Being called out is about the character of life we choose *in the world*, a counter-cultural life of service and sacrifice that emulates Jesus. We are agents of a kingdom not of this world that wants to break into this world. We display life in the presence of death, opening portals of light to push back the darkness. Our lives are meant to offer proof of the existence of another reality. The arena for this demonstration, Jesus made clear by his salt and light metaphors, is *in the world*.

The missional conversation helps us see this complete picture. It is helping the church in North America recover from missional amnesia. Missional theology champions a strategy of engaging the culture rather than retreating from it. This allows us to expand the bandwidth of how we think church gets expressed *in the world*. It provides the theological underpinning and backdrop for the newly unfolding storyline for church as missional community.

The Missional Church

The missional concept of church can be characterized as "the people of God partnering with him in his redemptive mission in the world." Every phrase of this description is critical for missional understanding.

The People of God

Seeing the church as *the people of God* allows for two significant and foundational insights. First, this understanding acknowledges the fact that the church is part of a larger meta-narrative that begins with Abraham's story. "The people of God" is used throughout scripture to point to a very special relationship in the central drama of the Bible. The saga begins with the call of Abraham, extends through Israel in the Old Testament, and unfolds into the church of the New Testament. This phrase is the language of relationship, not of institution or programming. It means that the church is a "who," not a "what" or an "it." Seeing church this way allows for the church to express itself in many different ways, not just in traditional congregational forms. We will return to this truth later in this chapter.

A second key insight into what it means to be *the people of God* comes right out of Abraham's call and mission. At the heart of the Abraham chronicle is the covenant that God makes with him. The account of this in Genesis 12 reveals the creation of a people on special assignment: to bless the world. This understanding of what it means to be the people of God provides the character of the church's interface with the world. Our communities and the people we come in contact with are supposed to be better off because of us!

The Old Testament recounts the drama of the people of God through slavery and redemption, captivity and release, times of leaning toward God and periods of running away from him. Throughout the drama the constant theme is God's pursuit of his people. The New Testament picks up on this theme by exploding the truth that God incarnates himself to come on mission in the person of Jesus. Jesus's spiritual descendents replaced Abraham's physical offspring as the new covenant people of God. This means that people of every tribe, every tongue, and every nation became part of the story line (Revelation 4).

Partnering with God

Though God can lay claim to all peoples of the earth, he has created a people with the responsibility of *partnering with him* as he pursues his work in the world ("Although the whole earth is mine, you will be for me a kingdom of priests and a holy nation." Exod. 19:5, NIV).

God is the primary missionary. He is the one who has been The Seeker since the Garden of Eden. The mission has been under way since Adam and Eve, well before Abraham and the creation of a covenant people. In other words there was a mission before there was the church. The church did not invent the mission nor does it have exclusive rights to it. Those belong to God. Said another way, the church does not have a mission; the mission has a church.

Why does God need a partner? The simple answer is, he doesn't. So why does God create a partner people? Two reasons seem apparent. The first is that God has a preference for incarnation when it comes to revealing his nature and intention. God prefers to work through people when possible. Abraham is blessed to show the world God's intention for all humanity. His offspring embody the story of God's redemptive efforts. Then ultimately God chooses to wrap himself in human flesh in Jesus.

Second, God creates a partner people because it is simply more fun for him this way. God loves to show off! Creation is proof enough. Having people acknowledge his efforts and recognize his work flat out jazzes him. (He even compliments himself when there was no one else to do it—"that's good" appears throughout the creation narrative and is an example of God high-fiving himself!)

Maybe we can understand God's thrill at creating a partner people if we reflect on some of our own experiences. Our enjoyment of a great restaurant discovery is made even more fabulous if we can later take others there. When they also have a great experience, our own satisfaction is heightened. The same dynamic holds true when we visit a place that we really fall in love with and scheme to bring others there to experience what we enjoy so much. Our own joy is magnified if we get to introduce others to this special place. And any of us with children know how much more fun Christmas is when it is celebrated with kids who are reveling in it.

This is the dynamic God experiences. He has "cut us in on the deal" so he can share with us what he is up to. In the process his own joy is magnified. The writer of Hebrews even speaks of Jesus's passion in these terms—"who, for the joy set before him endured the cross, scorning its shame, and sat down at the right hand of the throne of God" (Hebrews 12:2b, NIV). What was the joy in front of him? That he would get to take us to his favorite place, a place he had promised to his disciples ("I am going there to prepare a place for you. And if I go and prepare a place for you, I will come back and take you to be with me that you also may be where I am" [John 14:2b-3, NIV]). This thought surely crowded into Jesus's mind when he woke up in the tomb!

Those of us who are aware of God's mission in the world grow accustomed to God sightings, though we never grow accustomed to the God who is behind them. We get to see resurrections of hope and life and love. Everything else pales in comparison to the work of God we see all around us. And he is pleased that we notice!

A Redemptive Mission

The mission of God is a *redemptive mission*. Everything that sin broke is being addressed and restored through God's mission. This includes not just the ruptured relationship between God and humanity, but also the broken relationship of humans with themselves, among one another, and with the rest of creation.

The central act of redemption, the sacrifice of Jesus on the cross, graphically pictures the scope of the redemptive mission. The two beams of the cross reflect the dimensions of his redemptive work. The vertical beam reconnects people with their Creator. Sin ruptured our relationship with

God, the central relationship of our lives. The horizontal beam addresses the human plane of broken relationships affecting all aspects of our life on the planet. We are estranged from ourselves and from others. We do not conduct our relationships with the respect and integrity that we should. As opposed to serving and blessing others, we too often focus on getting ahead of them. Our relational dysfunction extends to the rest of creation, with our role as steward severely compromised.

Comprehending the full scope of God's redemptive work means that the church's mission cannot afford a false dichotomy in our understanding and pursuit of the gospel. Anything that diminishes life is sin. That means personal salvation is critical, but so too are issues of social justice and mercy. Dealing with institutional racism and poverty must be addressed along with a restoration of right standing with God. One cannot be complete without the other. After all, one side of a coin alone does not constitute a real coin; it is counterfeit without both sides.

The missional church acknowledges both dimensions of redemption. "Speaking the truth in love" (Ephesians 4:15, NIV) combines the two as one action, inseparable. We do not truly serve people if we withhold from them the truth about their condition and the hope that Jesus offers. However, people will not hear a message of love delivered by angry people through bullhorns and loudspeakers announcing judgment.

Redemption is a message that must be delivered by us on our knees holding a towel and basin. Acts of sacrifice and service will inevitably spark interest and lead to conversation. This is why followers of Jesus must be ready to give an answer for the hope that is in us (1 Peter 3:15). The apostle's admonition presumed that we would be queried. Increasingly, our engagement in redemptive pursuits will prompt those questions. Doing good sets the stage for God conversations with others, and followers of Jesus must not shrink back from these opportunities.

Partnering with God in his redemptive mission does not allow for a compartmentalization of life. We cannot wall off our engagements in the world from our spiritual lives. All of our relationships are arenas of spiritual formation, not just those with other followers of Jesus. All efforts to improve the quality of life for people are kingdom efforts, not just church activities, reflecting Jesus's promise that *abundant life* was the gift he brings. Shrinkwrapping God's interests down to church activity is not just ludicrous; it is idolatrous. Yet the North American church by and large continues to pursue a church-centric set of activities with church-centric metrics to evaluate its ministry success. Seeking the welfare of the people and places around us has up until now been off the screen of most congregations. But that is changing, thanks to the missional conversation.

In the World

The final phrase in the missional church description calls attention to the fact that the ministry platform and appropriate scorecard cannot be limited to church real estate and programming. The missional church shows itself and measures its effectiveness *in the world*. Jesus's prayer in the Garden of Gethsemane voiced his will that his followers, while being protected from the world, would remain in the world (John 17:15–18). He told Nicodemus that God so loved *the world* (John 3:16). The *world* is obviously in the cross-hairs of God's redemptive mission.

Unfortunately the church has too often slipped into a self-absorbed internal focus. Through the years the program church redefined the game to match its scorecard and was not willing to be accountable for its impact in the world, instead just focusing on church activity on church real estate. The result was that what it means to act as salt and light was changed into church members' being marketing agents for church membership or adopting a political and social agenda. "Abundant life" was contorted into church engagement. In the meanwhile, families are estranged, people go hungry, cynicism and fatalism hold hope hostage, and church leaders fret over meeting budgets and lament dwindling member support for an overstuffed church calendar.

The missional church conversation is calling the church to repent for the idolatrous behavior of placing ourselves above the world and to reengage the world as people who bless it. The obvious truth is that because the world is in God's heart it should also be in ours. Paul's analogy of the church as the bride of Christ surely is instructive at this point. People who enjoy healthy marriages care about those things that capture their spouse's attention. This is part of the dynamic when two become one. If we claim to be the people of God we cannot ignore whatever captures the heart of God. And God's heart is captured by the world.

A missional church casts its lot with the world. A church that thinks it is doing well in a city that is doing poorly is fooling itself. A radical recalibration of priorities is in order for many congregations. Raising high school graduation rates and lowering sexual exploitation rather than building campaigns and membership increases might become metrics of interest when the church understands why it has been left in the world. Microeconomic development and life coaching might become the primary ways the church disciples people. These activities might be considered sidebar efforts in a program-driven church, undertaken only after church activities are fully funded with leadership, money, and energy. But that is not the case in the missional worldview.

When we finally realize that our existence is to improve the world, and not escape it, we will grasp that the church is not the point. The kingdom is the point. The reign of God is not restricted to church activity. The kingdom of God manifests itself in the world, invading enemy territory, to liberate those held captive by a life-diminishing kingdom of darkness.

When we think of the church as being the body of Christ in the world we continue to perpetuate a church-centric perspective. We will begin our thinking inside the church and strategize about expanding it outward. If, however, we think of the body of Christ in the world as being the church (a nuance that my friend Al Hirsch has suggested) we begin our thinking very differently. We begin in the world, looking for ways that God is moving. We search for the kingdom outcroppings where good is breaking out and triumphing over evil. Instead of creating a congregation, hoping to affect the world, we see the church distilling out from the swirl of God's Spirit mixing it up with the world. It condenses out of the mix of other-world and world. A kingdom-centric view of church doesn't start with its organization and worship services; it begins with organic relationships and service. This thinking seems more in line with what Jesus taught us to pray (Your *kingdom* come, not Your *church* come).

The missional conversation is not just changing the scorecard for the church, it is actually and fundamentally changing the game. Understanding church as *the people of God partnering with him in his redemptive mission in the world* allows for a much broader bandwidth of how the church expresses itself in the world. It allows the church to move beyond the congregational existence and practices. It lays the foundation for seeing church as missional community.

Church as Missional Community

Church as missional community rests on a number of convictions, all of which are supported by the missional conversation. These ideas are borne out in the stories of missional communities that you will read about in the rest of the book. Their applications vary and each approach to missional communities has its own distinctive expression. These concepts are mostly implicit in missional communities' development but we spell them out here to better understand the DNA of this new church life form.

Church Is a *Who* Not a *What*

Once church is understood fundamentally in its organic nature we can recover the essence of the movement we see in the New Testament and the first few centuries that followed the events recorded there. Seeing church as a *what* is seeing it as something outside ourselves, something we go to, a place where certain things happen, a vendor of religious goods and services, something we support, something we invite people to attend. This is the predominant view of church that undergirds the understanding of church as congregation.

Seeing church as a *who*, however, means that wherever the body of Christ is, the church is present. This is the view of church incarnated in missional communities. Missional followers of Jesus think of church more as a verb rather than a noun. Church is not just an activity, it is a way of being in the world. Jesus followers church at work, at home, at school, in the neighborhood, in their leisure activities, in their altruistic engagement, even at church! Missional followers of Jesus view life as a mission trip. They serve as kingdom agents in every part of their life.

Grasping this organic and incarnational understanding of church challenges our institutional mind-set of church.

Instead of planting "a" church, we are always sowing "the" church. Rather than asking whether or not a missional community is "a" church, the right question is how it is being "the" church. This subtle language shift carries huge implications. It really reflects what we think we are up to. Planting or building or growing "a" church is an enterprise. Nurturing "the" church is a lifestyle, a way of being in the world, a sense of calling that provides a distinct identity for every follower of Jesus in every sphere of life, not just a descriptor of a certain set of group activities.

Almost every discussion of church in my lifetime has focused on a prescribed set of activities—fellowship, worship, prayer, evangelism, discipleship—all typically claiming to be patterned after the church in the book of Acts rather than focusing on the core DNA of what it means to *be* church. Sadly, these "functions" actually *are* what church means for many church leaders and members. These church activities certainly typify those things that followers of Jesus do but a person can adopt all these behaviors and still not be a follower of Jesus. It could be that a person just has been raised in a church culture or enjoys the social connections of a faith community. Surely the DNA of church has something to do with following the call of Jesus, being connected with him and with his mission in the world!

Understanding church as a *who* focuses and preserves the relational and connectional DNA of being part of the body of Christ. Missional communities highlight this aspect of church; after all, *community* is at the heart of this expression as well as *mission*.

Hanging Together

Some might wrongly conclude that seeing church as a *who* simply promotes individualism, that it just focuses on a personal connection with Jesus to the exclusion of how this plays out with others. This is an unwarranted conclusion. It is impossible to be connected with Christ's body without being organically connected to other parts of the body. This is precisely why Paul chose this metaphor to explain the church. In North America we have developed a consumer church culture in which a person can opt in or out of fellowship and can even live in a hostile relationship with other "members" without being called out or challenged to biblical standards of how we are to relate to one another in the body of Christ.

Let's be clear. There is no such animal as a privatized follower of Jesus because God exists in community. Trinitarian DNA runs through Jesus's blood and his blood flows through his body. The passionate drive for community gets passed along with the DNA of Jesus to those who are connected to him. Jesus's followers seek community, even create it. I have never met a genuine follower of Jesus who is not in search of other followers of Jesus to hang out with.

The formation of missional community, then, is a very natural and organic process. It stands in sharp contrast to what we typically refer to as church "planting." Though "planting" sounds organic our practices have been more like franchising or plug-and-play replication. Church planting in the Western culture has often involved starting a worship service, then trying to replicate a congregational organizational model. Planting a network of missional communities as the new church expression seems different only because the congregational church paradigm is so ensconced in our thinking and experience.

In the congregational modality of church, the key affinity uniting people might reside in ecclesiastical polity or program methodology. People join congregations because they like the way they function, because they agree with what they believe, or they like their ministry program.

In missional communities, the key affinity is mission. Missional affinity is approached in two basic ways, with some mixing and matching. Some communities primarily see themselves as having a mission together—a common cause that they feel called to give their lives to (serving the homeless, mentoring school children, adopting people groups, and so on). The missional community in these cases *is* the missionary. Other missional communities mainly see their group as a community *of* missionaries, each living intentionally in their life assignments, drawing encouragement and nurture for their mission from the missional community they are a part of. These communities might serve in projects together but they do not see the group as their major missional engagement with the world. Their lives are their mission trips.

The two essential components that provide the relational Velcro for all missional communities are their defined missional focus and the intentional community life they practice.

Missional Community Rhythms

We have already observed that many people's spiritual journeys are no longer congregational centered or congregational friendly. In the congregational modality people "go to church" to be engaged in worship, teaching, fellowship, and service with other Jesus followers. The assumption underlying this approach is that the congregation creates opportunities for spiritual growth, much of which is practiced in the church setting and expressed through participation in church programming. Much of this programming occurs every week. Most congregations go through an entire business cycle every seven days.

Missional communities often follow a different rhythm. For instance, many of the communities have a monthly cycle, not a weekly one. One week they may focus on worship, on another they may serve together in the community. Yet another week might be devoted to some specific life-skill training, and a fourth week might involve having a "Levi" party where community participants invite their pre-Christian friends to meet Jesus by hanging out with their Jesus-follower friends.

The content of the weekly gathering of the missional community also differs substantially in its rhythms from typical congregational program churches. In the latter a fairly defined schedule moves people from Bible study into worship with some scripted fellowship interface on a Sunday morning, often augmented with a mid-week activity of some sort, such as a small-group gathering. In missional communities the schedule tends to be much more flexible, taking its cues from the participants. Eating together frequently provides the central activity, with the community's focus sometimes being determined by what surfaces during the meal. If the life situation of one of the participants garners the lion's share of the community's attention, there is no sense of having upset the schedule or program. There is no obligation to cover a lesson, get through the liturgy, or process through a prescribed set of activities. The gathering is not program-centric; it is life-centric. People *are* the program!

Whereas worship and teaching are the major convening elements of church as congregation, in missional communities' fellowship, life debriefing, and service fuel the core rhythms. In congregations the focus of the weekly gathering is on what happens in the gathering, with much preparation during the week for the service, the class, whatever. (One Episcopal priest I corresponded with this week estimated that 30 percent of all clergy time in his congregation was spent in worship preparation, with clergy salaries consuming 60 percent of the church budget.)

In missional communities the focus of the gathering is on what happens away from the gathering. Everyday life is the core curriculum. The gathering celebrates and debriefs the participants' lives and missional engagement with the people around them. Worship and teaching are carried out against that backdrop. Worship leading is pretty simple and often passed around. Spontaneity in worship is fairly common, as opposed to prescribed liturgy or elements, although scripture reading is common. Some communities are blessed with musical talent, so their worship might heavily favor singing and other musical expressions. Less musically talented communities often import music into the community through iPods. Some communities worship with the larger Christian community on some rhythm, perhaps at Easter and Christmas or more frequently.

Stories of God sightings from everyday life are recounted in missional community gatherings. Breakthroughs in life behavior and insight are rehearsed. Many communities practice smaller group interfaces where in-depth relationship building, Bible study, or life debriefing occurs. Some do this in pairs, others in triads, and others where the missional community itself numbers several dozen have small groups. Many communities have established protocols for keeping in touch with each other during the week, whether through social media or personal contact. Praying for one another is routine, informed by life needs that surface in community conversation as well as life experience.

People move in and out of missional communities. Some of this is due to the mobility of our culture. Sometimes the movement will be from a congregation into a missional community, for any number of reasons. At other times the flow will be in the opposite direction. The missional community I am a part of encouraged a young couple to become part of a program church for the sake of their children. Theirs was a special need that arose out of the parents' life situation, one in which the kids were isolated from other children during the week. Social needs along with spiritual considerations made this an obvious path for the children's development. Who knows? In a few years, this young family may choose to church again as a missional community.

Leadership Structure

The leadership structure of missional communities differs substantially from that of congregational church. Instead of layers of elders, pastors, and staff who make decisions and supervise programs, deliver pastoral care, lead worship, and teach, missional communities are served by a much flatter leadership structure. Leadership reflects a distributive model, which is a fancy way of saying that leadership is simple and shared. In most missional communities all are expected to contribute, whether in food preparation, discussion, cleaning up, child care, praying, sharing, or whatever.

The missional community culture does not require clergy leadership. Teaching does not play the central role in the gathering, so the community gathering does not rely on a theologically trained clergy person. This does not signal that biblical teaching is devalued; it is just deemphasized as the major convening element. Teaching often is imported into the community from podcasts or books produced by theologically trained teachers or the teachings of the pastors of congregations that the missional community is attached to. The key leadership role (which, again, may or may not reside in a single individual) is that of facilitating community life, making sure that the various community functions of serving, hospitality, and spiritual formation are all accomplished. Leadership for various tasks typically flows to the person(s) most gifted and most interested in those functions.

Every missional community system you encounter in the following pages takes leadership development very seriously. For most it begins with some kind of apprentice training. Leaders typically are indigenous to the group, the neighborhood, and the project. Missional community leaders also attend systematic training, usually on a monthly or biweekly schedule, along with annual retreats and quarterly specialized trainings. Personalized coaching is available in most of the missional community cultures detailed in this book. The source of training and coaching varies according to the missional community's context. In some cases, church staff leaders have assigned duties that include this area of responsibility. Whatever the system, lots of peer learning occurs when missional community leaders debrief their experiences with one another.

Much of the focus of leadership training is on the personal and spiritual development of the leader. In missional communities leadership resides in the person, not in a position. In the traditional congregational church, leadership is usually gauged in terms of organizational effectiveness and professional abilities, including the competencies necessary to create and manage church programs. In missional communities leadership effectiveness is tied to the development of people and the competencies that are required to be an effective coach for life issues and soul nurturing. Character, personality, and judgment of leaders are under greater scrutiny. Whereas many people in congregations do not encounter their leaders outside of their ministry platform and duties, the missional community sees the leader in all kinds of life settings. This means that the leader's relational intelligence, as well as personal abilities, factor into his or her effectiveness.

Some critics of missional communities have asserted that this form of church life is a rebellion against spiritual authority. This misunderstanding is at best uninformed; at worst it is fueled by a perpetuation of the need for a clergy-dominated structure—a control need that is psychological, not theological or biblical. After all, the church did quite well in its early centuries before the rise of a clergy class. Spiritual authority is not unimportant in missional communities. The authority of the Spirit and the scriptures is practiced often in ways that church as congregation can escape. In missional communities, for instance, whether participants live out the truth is under far greater scrutiny than in the typical congregational setting. Personal accountability is a hallmark of missional communities, not just for leaders, but for everyone.

No Template

What you will see in each of the accounts that follow reveals the variety of approaches to missional communities. There is no template for how they are formed, the rhythms they choose, the way they are positioned with regard to other church structures, how big they are, or the exact way they engage with the community around them. There is no one-size-fits-all model of plug-and-play missional community.

This diversity reflects the organic nature of church as missional community. The soil determines what life it will support; in this case, the soil is the combination of the people involved and the particular goals and strategies of the missional impetus that gives rise to the community. For instance, some strategies include more of a network architecture. In this case the church sees itself as a network of missional communities, not a gathered congregation. In other instances, missional communities reside within a congregational structure, providing a new way for members to engage in missional service and spiritual formation.

The variety of form and function of missional communities also signals a reality that this new life expression faces a steep learning curve. We are in the early development of this church life form. Lots of experimentation is taking place. As the knowledge base grows we will likely see more site and situation–neutral learnings that can be easily transferred into and grafted on all varieties of life in the missional community garden.

New Technology

To employ another metaphor, what we are seeing in the rise of missional communities is the development of a parallel or alternative technology for church as congregation.

The arrival of any new technology inevitably involves disruption to existing approaches as well as developmental hiccups. Progress can be uneven. Many early adopters do not experience what they expect. Early adapters eventually ensure that the new technology finds its way into widespread use. Late adopters and adapters might even apply the new technology to other applications unanticipated in the initial development. (The web, for example, was initially created for academics to share papers through hypertext.)

An insightful analogy of missional communities might come from the oil industry. Oil companies have perfected the technology required to process oil that is found in the readily accessible pools floating under the surface of some countries, especially in the Middle East. After decades of application these refinery processes are efficient and consistent. However, billions more gallons of oil are trapped inside of oil sands.

It is highly diffused rather than concentrated and is deeply embedded inside of other elements. The technology required to extract and refine this oil differs significantly from the processes used in standard, easy-to-get-to oil reserves.

The church-as-congregation modality knows how to locate and process people who are susceptible to being "church people." We have had centuries of congregational application to figure out how best to do this, from exploring new fields and drilling exploratory wells (church planting) to getting additional yields out of existing wells (church renewal). These processes will continue, though we have observed that the population reserves susceptible to this technology are drying up. This does not mean, nor do I suggest, that church as congregation should be mothballed. There's still a lot of life there.

What I *am* declaring, however, is that millions of people who cannot be processed by church as congregation remain potential fields for church as missional community. These people are deeply embedded into a culture that is rapidly moving away from traditional spiritual practices and organizational forms of religious pursuit. Yet they are wide open to a new technology that comes alongside their life rhythms rather than requiring them to adopt a new lifestyle and rhythm to match existing church practice.

To push the analogy a bit further, the technology for getting oil sands and shale oil is being developed by the major oil companies. When a barrel of oil reaches a certain price point or when existing reserves are depleted, these companies will be ready to go after these oil reserves. It would be irresponsible and poor business for the oil companies to delay the exploration and development of these parallel technologies until we are out of oil! And it would be silly for Exxon Mobil to see the development of these new oil-processing technologies as threatening to its current processes. Exxon Mobil doesn't see its business model tied to only one way of processing oil. It sees itself in the energy business, so it is exploring all kinds of alternative fuels and processes to meet the world's energy needs.

The exploration and development of missional communities provide a way forward for the church. If church leaders think we are in the "church-as-congregation" business, then our model is tied to one technology. This business model narrowly defines church by traditional congregational practices and metrics. This approach destines us to be out of business in terms of being able to connect with increasing numbers of people in our culture. If, however, we see ourselves as partners with God in his redemptive mission, we acknowledge that we are in the kingdom enterprise, a perspective that allows for all kinds of innovation and new life.

Seeing missional communities as a new technology means that their development can serve as a key strategy of existing congregations to engage their mission fields. Many congregations could operate several dozens to even hundreds of missional communities under the umbrella of their existing ministries. The impact would not be registered in the typical congregational metrics focusing on worship service attendance or program participation. However, people who will never be church people could encounter the gospel.

After all, we are talking about something way more critical than oil production. We are talking about people who need the hope that Jesus uniquely offers them for experiencing abundant life.

The Stories

The stories of missional communities chosen for inclusion in this book have been selected to illustrate the varieties of shape and structure of this new life form. Missional communities are proving to be very adaptable to a wide range of environments and can serve diverse purposes. The approaches we look at in the pages that follow give us a look at missional communities functioning as

- A way to establish presence in every crack and crevice of a nonchurch culture (European missional communities)
- An organizing architecture for the network church (Soma Communities)
- An evangelism strategy for hard-to-reach people groups (UT Austin)
- An outreach strategy for megachurches (Future Travelers)
- A vehicle for spiritual formation and community transformation (Mission Houston)

The accounts are not designed to be prescriptive—"this is how you do it"—but rather to present a diverse sample of the new life form that is being cultivated in various ways in different ecologies. I have made no attempt to "harmonize" the various approaches. Some of them offer competing voices and some are complementary. I have not imposed a structure for telling the stories. Instead, I have tried to let the players speak in their own voices so that we can grasp what it is that drives them and what they are trying to accomplish in their setting. I have refrained from any deconstruction, critical analysis, or opinions of what I like or don't like about these various approaches. I leave that to you as you consider the possible variations of this new life form you want to plant in your church garden.

These experiments are works-in-progress. They have made some changes from the time I chronicled their story to the time you are reading it. We don't know how all this is going to turn out. But that's the point! We are on the front end of something that is emerging before our very eyes. My hope is that the telling of these stories will excite your imagination. Perhaps you will help us figure out church as missional community as we move forward into this new post-congregational expression of God's ongoing mission.

Let's get started!

3

MISSIONAL COMMUNITIES— EUROPEAN STYLE

Mike Breen began to tinker with the idea of missional communities late in the 1980s while serving as an Anglican priest in a very poor section of London called Brixton. He took the small group ministry model (primarily charged with pastoral care and discipleship) and infused it with missional intentionality. These small groups of eight to fifteen people were early iterations of missional communities. Breen says that he learned several things from these early days of experimentation. Positively, he learned that lay-led ministry worked and that the "lightweight and low maintenance" small-group structure allowed for easy support and reproduction. On the downside, he realized that the groups were "small enough to care, but not large enough to dare." Maintaining momentum was an issue and leadership burnout was common.

In 1994 Breen became senior pastor ("team rector") of St. Thomas in Sheffield, England, and began to push the missional community concept further. The church began to gather multiple small groups together to form *clusters* (the original term for missional communities) of twenty to fifty people to participate in a common mission. The clusters were tasked to find a "crack or crevice of society" and incarnate the gospel to that specific culture. The result, Breen says, was that people "who would never darken the door of a church in a million years" started coming to faith in Christ.

Over time, people began to prefer these larger gatherings for mission even more than their small-group experiences and started to hang out more in the clusters. Identity began forming around these mid-size groups, described by Breen as a sort of extended family. The communities began reproducing.

The sustainability of these missional communities proved itself in a time of church crisis. The church building became suddenly uninhabitable. An electrical problem rendered the building unsafe, presenting no option other than to demolish the structure. At that point, with no building in the city large enough to house the megacongregation, Breen recalls, "our community was suddenly homeless and there wasn't anywhere we could meet every week."

A bold plan was conceived and implemented. The congregation was assigned across the city to these mid-sized groups of missional communities. Congregational members were told that their primary identity was going to be their missional community, with the whole church coming together only once a month for a "normal" worship service. For a year the church functioned primarily as missional communities. When a building was secured that could house the multiple services of the church, church leaders made a remarkable discovery. The church had not just grown during the year's time; it had doubled!

Rather than resume "business as normal" church leaders decided to continue to keep energy flowing toward the missional communities and the multiplication of missional communities continued. Breen gives a partial list of cultures that saw missional communities form: the creative class, former gang members, former Iranian Muslims, university students, former prostitutes and drug addicts, new parents, multiple neighborhoods, and the homeless population. In a city where less than 1 percent of people attend church, many were now experiencing the gospel through these missional communities. When the scattered church gathered to worship, Mike recalls, the resulting diversity testified to the reach of the missional communities. "Every color, age, race, and religious background" pictured the coming kingdom.

St. Thomas Sheffield became a multi-site church in the first decade of the twenty-first century. St. Thomas Philadelphia (St. Thomas Philly) is the more urban and network model, with missional communities serving as its core expression. Rich Robinson serves as the missional communities team leader of that congregation, with primary responsibility for overseeing the work of over a hundred missional communities. St. Thomas Crookes (site of the original St. Thomas Sheffield) is the more suburban and hybrid model congregation, with a highly attractional worship ministry augmented with missional communities as an outreach strategy. Tom Finnemore, the minister to university students on that staff, has found that missional communities are a very effective strategy for engaging college students, who are easy to motivate into mission. Still using the "cluster" designation, Tom observes that many college students view their cluster as their primary church identity.

This trilogy—Breen, Robinson, and Finnemore—will speak in this chapter for the St. Thomas missional community experience of yesterday and today. Breen now exports the movement through his 3D ministry based in Pawleys Island, South Carolina.

Breen has also been a catalytic leader in the European Church Planting Network (ECPN), an initiative of Leadership Network. Working with Brent Dolfo, the Leadership Network director of the project, and about twenty church planting teams, the ECPN since 2007 has helped to plant over one thousand congregations with the missional community DNA. This remarkable development has occurred in countries like Germany, Switzerland, Norway, and Latvia. In this chapter I have included the story of one application of missional community on the Continent—Valgmenighed Church in Aarhus, Denmark. I have done this to demonstrate the portability of this life form and to show how missional communities are proving to be an effective strategy for incarnational ministry in the post-congregational European culture.

Mike calls attention to an early decision he made at St. Thomas Sheffield. He went to the church after it had endured a well-publicized church scandal in the United Kingdom. He found a culture badly in need of establishing accountability in terms of growing disciples, not just spectators and church consumers. The "huddle" strategy you will read about in this chapter for training missional community leaders was actually the accountability and discipleship strategy for church members first developed to address the key issue confronting Mike at St. Thomas. Mike's reflection on this new discipleship vehicle as a "game-changer" is worth noting. "Most people who hear our story are most intrigued by what we accomplished with missional communities," he says. "But, truth be told, none of that happens without having a strong discipling culture. What we found was that discipleship is often the missing link to create a missional church. We found that if you actually create disciples who know how to do mission, you'll get the missional thing."

Key Definitions

The four key components to the cluster development at Sheffield—adapted in the other European network church applications—are the missional community, huddle, up-in-out dimensions of ministry, and the "person of peace" strategy.

Missional Community

In their *Launching Missional Communities: A Field Guide* (3DM, 2010), Mike Breen and Alex Absalom identify what they call the "bare essentials" for missional communities:

- A group of between twenty and fifty people (at the most seventy)
- Can be a new church plant or, more commonly, be part of a network of missional communities that are part of a larger gathered church
- Has a defining focus on reaching a particular neighborhood or network of relationships
- Often revolves around shared times of food and fun
- Maintains a healthy balance of up-in-out ministry dimensions
- Includes non-Christians
- Conducts worship, prayer, and scripture reading as core practices
- Keeps an outward focus through a mixture of service and verbal witness
- Gathers informally through the week
- Creates small cell group experiences for support, challenge, and closeness in members' lives together

- Is led by lay leaders who receive ongoing coaching and have a high degree of accountability to the missional community and their coaches
- Share leadership and service responsibilities among all members of the missional community
- Reproduce into other missional communities

Missional communities are not stand-alone entities in the St. Thomas system. They "orbit the celebration," according to Rich Robinson (*celebration* is the term used for the gathered church in worship). Missional communities are not *in spite of* or *in place of* the gathered church. "There has to be some connection to the base, even if it is only a leadership connection," Rich added. This connection is essential for accountability and can be one way the missional community is distinguished from a stand-alone house church. At St. Thomas Philly missional communities attend Sunday worship once or twice a month, though the non-Christians typically don't attend the Sunday gatherings.

Huddle

A huddle is a group of missional community leaders who meet for discipleship, training, and accountability. The huddle typically meets every other week. The emphasis of the exchange between huddle participants and the huddle leader is on learning to hear the voice of God and practicing obedience to what one hears. Two questions often frame the discussion: *what is God saying to me?* and *how will I respond?* The huddle not only includes current leaders with missional community assignments, but is also designed to produce more leaders by including people who show leadership potential and missional readiness. Huddles have specific durations, with the ultimate goal of having huddle members recruit their own huddle groups. Participation in the huddle is by invitation only. Its focus on leadership development separates it from being just another small group.

Up-In-Out

Jesus modeled a balanced missional life with the three dimensions of up-in-out. His deep and connected relationship to his Father and his attentiveness to the Spirit's direction reflect the up dimension. Jesus's constant investment in the disciples' development demonstrated the in dimension. He attended to the out dimension in his redemptive mission to the world, which included personal implications as well as systemic issues (for example, racism and injustice).

Breen contends that missional communities are called to reflect on these same three dimensions in their ministry and life together. The up dimension includes worship and efforts toward helping members maintain a dynamic and growing relationship with God, including a personal relationship with Jesus as Savior. Typical in-dimension emphases of community life are the nurture and care of each other, praying for one another, encouraging one another, and attending to the physical, social, economic, and spiritual needs of other members. Out-dimension expressions of service and witness vary from group to group, depending on the particular mission of the community. Some communities target the homeless and others minister in night clubs, some in gated communities, and others convene Alpha groups in their living rooms and office conference centers.

Leaders in the Sheffield church make several observations about how the up-in-out dimensions play out in community life. Rich Robinson notes that at any given time missional communities follow a leading beat—worship, discipleship, or service will be more pronounced for a period. "You can't do it all every time, each time," he observes. "One dimension will be emphasized for a while before the rhythm of the community shifts to another leading beat."

Tom Finnemore of St. Thomas Crookes comments that the third expression (up-in-out) of a missional community typically reflects the particular gifting of the leader, especially as it relates to the fivefold ministry of apostle, prophet, evangelist, pastor, and teacher (identified in Ephesians 4). Apostolically gifted leaders will tend to focus on the out dimension, for instance, and pastor types will naturally gravitate to in-dimensional emphases. Because of these tendencies leaders must possess self-awareness and be committed to accountability for leading the missional community in all three dimensions. An important strategy for balance involves building a leadership team that reflects all aspects of the fivefold gifting.

Mike Breen came to some early conclusions about the interface of these three dimensions and missional intentionality of groups. He observed that groups that started either with an up-and-in (emphasis on worship and discipleship) or an in-and-up (strong fellowship and teaching) focus had great difficulty developing an outward dimension to their ministry. However, he found that groups that began with a strong out dimension had less difficulty transitioning to the other two dimensions of healthy group life.

The Person of Peace

In Luke 9 and 10, Matthew 10, and Mark 6, Jesus gives an often-overlooked strategy for our gaining entrance and winning favor with a community that we are attempting to penetrate with the gospel. He admonished his disciples to find a person of peace who would serve as a gatekeeper to allow them passage into the community. The person of peace is someone who welcomes you, serves you, and responds to you. Most likely a personal bond can be established and developed into a relationship that eventually opens up a whole network of relationships. This approach to evangelism proves organic and relationally rich. God prepares the person of peace for your arrival. Seeking this person is a way of partnering with the pre-evangelistic work of the Spirit.

The Four Spaces—Anthropology and Church Practice

Missional communities play a vital role in helping the church make use of "space," but not in terms of physical facilities (although they do allow a church to expand without constructing new buildings). The space under consideration here is the relational space that people inhabit.

Anthropologist Edward T. Hall pioneered the understanding of "proxemics" or how people use space, particularly in their communication with others (*The Hidden Dimension*, Anchor Books/Doubleday, 1966). Proxemics recognizes four spaces:

- *Intimate distance (zero to eighteen inches)*. This is the arena of play wrestling and love-making, where people share their deepest and most personal thoughts and emotions. This space is inhabited by people who feel drawn to each other.

- *Personal distance (eighteen inches to four feet)*. At eighteen inches we move from our territorial bubble into personal space. People are at arm's length, ready to be embraced, held, or shoved away. Where people stand in this space indicates their level of closeness.

- *Social distance (four feet to ten feet)*. This is the zone of impersonal transaction. We rely only on what we see and hear for communication because we have moved past the distance where the senses of touch and smell inform our communication. At the outer edges of this distance, beyond eight feet, it is easy to disengage from conversation with others.

- *Public distance (ten feet to infinity)*. This is the space of lecture halls and mass meetings. Shared experiences in this space rely on something outside the personal contact between individuals, such as a teacher, speaker, or drama production.

These distances vary from culture to culture. Although the boundaries listed here prove accurate in American culture, other cultures—like some in Europe and Asia—allow people to come in much closer before there is a sense of violation of personal space.

What does all this have to do with missional communities? According to Breen, it provides a critical understanding of their social and spiritual dynamics. "Now all this talk about distances is not some abstract theory ... because this idea defines what we do and do not do in distinct places" (*Launching Missional Communities*, p. 44). In other words, the "distances" in proxemics create four "spaces" that allow distinct activity and levels of communication and relationships.

Public space, for instance, is where the gathered church practices celebration—the "Sunday" services—where people are mostly connected through something outside themselves, the delivery of teaching, drama, and music by leaders and performers. Church small-group ministries inhabit the *personal space*, where groups of three to twelve people meet for Bible study, fellowship, even some ministry tasks that are mutually agreed on and voluntarily engaged in. *Intimate space* can only be inhabited by one or two other people. This is where genuine accountability occurs. These relationships can be encouraged but not forced; they rely on mutual assent and invitation.

Missional communities, Breen asserts, play an important role in restoring *social space* in the church. This is the arena that up to several dozen people can inhabit—an extended family or *oikos* (Greek for *household*)—where they experience community life, practice their shared values, debrief their personal experiences, and establish identity. And, most critically, they are able to engage the world on intentional mission with the gospel. This latter capacity separates the missional community from being just a small-group experience because most small-group experiences focus on the in and up dimensions, not the out dimension. European Church Planting Network missional community literature says missional communities are "small enough to have a common vision, but big enough to do something about it" ("Mid-Sized Mission: The Use of Mid-Sized Groups as a Vital Strategic Component of Church Planting"—ECPN concept paper, 2008).

When churches and church leaders don't understand these various spaces they fail to adequately provide for various levels of belonging that people need. People looking for possible connections in safe environments need the public space to explore this possibility. The attractional worship gathering provides for this need.

But beyond this, many congregations begin to promote and even promise a level of intimacy that they are not designed structurally to provide. Many people are dissatisfied with their small-group experiences precisely at this point. The idea that meeting together with a dozen other people engaged in some common practices will provide deep intimacy is an unrealistic expectation. People can't sustain intimacy at that level. Only a few people can occupy the intimate space of our lives. This cannot be forced and only happens at the cellular level of heart-to-heart, life-on-life engagement. This is why many models of discipleship make the case that triads and quartets are optimum for life transformations (see Greg Ogden's *The New Reformation* and Neil Cole's LTGs—life transformation groups—detailed in *Organic Church* and other of Cole's writings).

Even if public space and intimate space are provided for, and churches figure out the exact role of small groups in their delivery of personal space relationships, the need for social space remains. People need a group to belong to that is capable of having good parties and engaging in some projects beyond the group. Social space provides a web of relationships that establishes identity and a sense of personal belonging that lies in between the consumer-spectator place and the heart-to-heart place. This is where missional communities come in.

Rich Robinson at St. Thomas Philly positions the four relationship spaces and numbers of people as follows: a person's covenant group will have two to three people; a cell will contain five to nine members; a community (or congregation in Breen's parlance) will involve nine to thirty participants; and groups of thirty or more create celebration-size groups. The missional communities "orbit" the celebration and do not exist "in place of" or "in spite of" the center. Not every missional community has covenant and cell components; that depends on the make-up of the community itself. Those spaces in peoples' lives may be addressed in other settings.

Leaders of missional communities may encounter tensions related to these people spaces. Some people coming into the community will bring pressure to take the group down to the small-group level, where they can practice a level of sharing and intimacy that cannot be sustained with a group of twenty or more people. "Thus, running an MC [missional community] like a small group is a sure inhibitor for any sort of growth. Instead, we should always break down into small groups (personal spaces) to share private thoughts, needs, and requests" (*Launching Missional Communities*, p. 47).

Missional community leaders, Breen suggests, should act "up" rather than down. Once the size of the group reaches the teens it is better to begin to operate as if the group contained twenty-five people or more. In fact, he insists that inviting more people to join the missional community needs to be "the" top priority for the group at this point. Otherwise it will succumb to gravitational forces that keep it from being able to function effectively. "The danger of a group settling at twelve to eighteen people is that it will operate like a big small group and won't have the resources and momentum for effective mission" (*Launching Missional Communities*, p. 47). When training leaders, Breen encourages them to aim for twenty people as a baseline to adequately address the social space dynamics.

So what is the optimum size of the missional community? Rich Robinson says they started with twenty to fifty people in mind as their desired size. However, they found that as the group approached forty it became hard to find lay leaders who could lead in their spare time and give adequate attention to the community. They also discovered that forming and maintaining relationships become very difficult at that size. They have settled in on fifteen to twenty-five as the optimum missional community size.

Once a group gets between twenty and twenty-five people the community is encouraged to begin thinking about what is next for them in terms of multiplying themselves. Some communities choose to send out two to three leaders to begin other groups and some communities dissolve and reemerge as two groups. St. Thomas Philly has grown to over 120 missional communities in this way.

Missional Community Formation and Rhythm

Missional communities do not work when people are just assigned to them. As extended households that inhabit social space, missional communities work off of shared vision and values. Rich at St. Thomas Philly says that vision is easier to connect with, but how it is lived out is the values piece. Values bring out the most conflict as people search for and agree on an intentional strategy for implementing vision. Missional communities need more emotional glue than that people simply like each other and want to hang out together. They require shared mission—vision and values—to thrive.

Getting to shared mission typically requires some coaching on a series of questions that help people identify their missional impulses. Two questions that guide the thinking at St. Thomas Philly are *who do you want to be good news to?* and *what would good news look like?* The leaders help people conduct what they call "passion audits" to get at this. They ask people about their hearts' desires—*what excites your heart?* But they also ask people about their holy discontent—*what breaks your heart?* They further engage people in conversations about where they think grace or peace is needed—such as certain neighborhoods or people groups—as well as where the opportunities are for missional engagement.

The missional targets generally start off as big ideas. Usually some coaching is required to help communities answer what it means or looks like to move into that space with missional intent. Some missional communities start with this all figured out. Most others move slowly into this through discovery, typically involving trial-and-error engagement with various projects and people groups. The process of coming to shared mission often reflects the personality and journey of the leader. Although some leaders create missional communities with the missional target already in mind, and thus recruit to the mission, others prefer to use the actual mission-defining process as one way to build community.

Missional communities meet in homes, cafes and restaurants, community centers, even church buildings, depending on the size of the community and their missional target. Some communities meet every week (like many of the two dozen missional communities of college students at St. Thomas Crookes) and others meet only twice a month. Some missional communities prefer to participate with the celebration service of the larger church at least once a month, some more often (at St. Thomas Philly it is expected that the group attend a Sunday celebration one weekend a month, with up to two more optional; for college students at St. Thomas Crookes there is a weekly service each Sunday evening at 7 PM, with celebration services being a large part of their outreach strategy to the two universities in the city). At least one weekend or Sunday a month is used by the missional community as a mission day to work in the community with their target group. The leadership huddles typically alternate weeks with the gathering of the whole community.

A month in the life of a missional community might look something like the following rhythm:

Week One. Sunday celebration with gathered church. Community gathering midweek with accountability groups.

Week Two. Sunday celebration or missional community gathering. Midweek leadership huddle.

Week Three. Sunday celebration or missional community gathering. Midweek accountability groups.

Week Four. Mission day or weekend with target group. Midweek leadership huddle. Party night to invite friends and people of peace.

Of course, lots of informal interaction occurs between all of these scheduled gatherings and activities. The rhythm of the missional community is informed by the nature of their engagement with their target group and the life needs of community participants.

Missional communities do a variety of things in their gatherings. Breen notes that these elements vary according to the needs of the community and the rhythm of in-up-out. He also recommends that missional communities begin their out expression early in order to help gel the group (not waiting until the group members get to know each other better). Gatherings will include the following:

- Food, ideally sharing a meal together
- Socializing, having fun
- Sharing communion
- Storytelling, with community participants sharing their God encounters and personal thanksgivings
- Worship (something simple that is participatory and easy to prepare, not competing with the planning and scale of the larger-scale weekend celebrations)
- Prayer for particular needs or healing
- Studying the scriptures (with emphasis on hearing what the Spirit is saying through the passage and what people will do about it; designed to encourage obedience)

- Praying for the community at large and the people group or cause targeted in mission
- Planning for engagement with the external mission

Leaders of missional communities should keep in mind that the gatherings should be conducted in such a way that people who are not believers can participate and feel welcomed.

Another frequent issue for missional communities relates to how children are integrated into community life. Again there is no template for how this is addressed. Having a baby or two to pass around during the gathering doesn't present the same challenge as having half a dozen or more toddlers and preschoolers to figure out what to do with. Many young couples need some relief from parenting for a couple of hours while others are energized by the presence of children. Many groups wind up with a hybrid experience with part of the time being all-inclusive and part of the time being separated. Some groups bring in other people to help with the child-specific activities and other groups pass this responsibility around with shared leadership or swap services with other missional communities. When the children are included, it is important that they are really engaged, not just spectators. They can and should take age-appropriate roles of leadership and service as a part of their own personal and spiritual development.

As organic entities missional communities have life cycles. None are designed to last forever. Rich Robinson at St. Thomas Philly observes that they have found that missional communities generally last two to four years. This time frame results from a very important factor. "That is the time cycle of a good leader to raise up other leaders to create other missional communities," according to Rich.

Speaking of Leadership

Missional communities must be led by missional leaders. Recruiting and nurturing these leaders requires great intentionality.

Leadership Language

The commitment to developing leaders is part of the culture of missional communities. "Without the culture, missional communities are just another church structure," stresses Robinson. Breen and the St. Thomas network use some key phrases to describe their leadership philosophy and build their leadership culture.

Low Control, High Accountability

Ministry does not need to be controlled by those in power; rather, it needs to be released to people who have the vision for how they can minister to people in the name of Jesus. Rather than being at the center, control needs to be pushed to the edges where people are feeling the call of God to intersect their world with the gospel. People should have great freedom to dream about how God would use them in the world. This freedom should be exercised in a framework of high accountability. This includes accountability all the way around—to the ministry supervisors and coaches, to other missional community leaders, to group members, and to the target population. The leadership culture at St. Thomas sets a high bar of mutual accountability.

Lightweight and Low Maintenance

Too often churches and church leaders construct complex structures and approaches to ministry that require too much feeding. The missional community structure is simple and organic. The activities of the community should be kept simple and easy to do. For instance, Bible study needs to focus on what the Spirit is saying and not be dependent on someone with a theology degree to lead it. Engaging the target population or network of relationships needs to be done in a way that is as uncomplicated as possible. The goal is to release as much energy and resource into people as possible and not soak it all up with maintaining organizational needs. This approach can help prevent burnout among leaders, who typically are jazzed by engagement with people and their needs but drained by bureaucratic processes.

Everyone Can Play

Missional community leaders need to create a space where people can step forward and into their giftedness and calling. They don't need to do all the leading, serving, or strategizing. Others can and should participate in some level. This keeps people from feeling that ministry only belongs to the professionals or leaders. Everyone should have responsibility for the welfare and growth of the missional community. Having this attitude from the start helps sow the idea of multiplication into the community's DNA because there is the realization that leaders are being raised up at every level for their next assignment. This philosophy contributes to creating a movement and not building an institutional model in which only a few can give direction.

Leadership Requirements

Not everyone who wants to be a leader can be. There must be four things present—Breen calls these the 4 Cs—character, competency, chemistry, and capacity. These can be assessed by thinking through the following evaluative questions:

- *Are they committed to Christ?* This doesn't mean perfection but are there obvious problems, addictions, character issues that must be addressed?

- *Are they committed to our church?* This assesses whether the candidates are onboard with the church's approach to ministry as well as whether they plan to be around long enough to build and sustain meaningful relationships.

- *Do they have a clear mission vision?* Although this might take some coaching to tease out its specificity, leaders have to be broken or moved by something in order to be able to inspire others.

- *Are they willing to be accountable?* This means a firm commitment to participate in the leadership huddles and be a part of a team.

- *Will others follow them?* They should have proved that others will follow them at some level. Their following can be small or large but it needs to be present in some way.

The idea is not to disqualify as many people as possible but to raise up as many leaders as you can, knowing that people have varying capacities for leadership. Careful recruitment on the front end can avoid very painful and costly experiences later.

Ongoing Leadership Training

A team of volunteer seasoned missional community leaders serve as coaches in the St. Thomas Philly church. They convene the leadership huddles that form the basic delivery system for leadership development. The huddles meet twice a month and are really geared to the personal development of the leader as well as dealing with the leadership challenges that arise during the course of ministry. Missional community leaders are expected to be regular in their participation in these as well as other training opportunities. More formalized training occurs in special monthly leadership nights and leadership weekends that are scheduled every six months. These sessions are archived on the church website (www.stthomaschurch.org.uk/communities) and available for those who could not attend. Individual coaching from staff is also available. Finally, each missional community leader is expected to recruit a prayer team or network that supports their leadership efforts.

The Role of Staff

The role of church staff shifts in a church committed to a missional community architecture. First, if the church is truly missional, staff leaders are being expected more and more to spend their efforts in the community at large, not just at the church giving program direction and project management. This brings the staff into intersection more with community needs, which in turn intersects with the out-dimension work of the missional communities. Staff are involved in a number of other ways, from recruiting and coaching of missional community leaders to personal participation in missional community life. Depending on the number of missional communities a church has, some churches designate a staff role as the missional communities supervisor (Rich). Other churches make missional community supervision a major part of their staff assignment (Tom).

Valgmenighed Church—Aarhus Denmark

The missional community movement of the European Church Planting Network in many ways expresses the legacy of the work begun at St. Thomas Sheffield. To see the participants and some of their work go to www.ecpn.org. The Danish application is a good one because it reflects well the character of the movement.

Aarhus is the second-largest city in Denmark, numbering around 350,000 people (Copenhagen is the largest with around 1.5 million people). It is a college town, with between 40,000 and 50,000 college students. This fact shows up in the Valgmenighed Church in that its average age of member is thirty-one years old. This demographic differs remarkably from other congregations in Denmark, which has a Lutheran state church that has been in decline for decades, populated mostly by senior adults. Valgmenighed also is atypical in another regard: it is growing—at 14 percent per year since 2005. With seven hundred members it is one of the largest churches in the country. And this is only about half of the worshipping congregation, however, because membership represents a high-bar commitment. Becoming a member requires completing an eight-hour membership course plus having an interview with one of the ministry team.

This unusual growth, according to Sune Andersen, the church's executive pastor, results from its cluster (missional communities) strategy. Clusters do two things, according to Andersen. "They break the client-provider model, which creates an atmosphere of apathy." He explains that churches in Denmark with a handful of congregants can still maintain a full-time pastor and organist because of the 1-percent income tax that supports the church. Therefore, there is little incentive among the clergy to grow or expectation that the congregation will be meaningfully engaged with the life of the church. Andersen further observes that "clusters also raise the issue of what it means to be a disciple of Jesus—to be people of faith and make a difference in the community."

For the first ten years of its existence the church numbered around a hundred people, a fairly typical church in its approach to ministry employing the "client-provider" model. In 2003 then–senior pastor Anders-Michael Hansen journeyed to St. Thomas Sheffield to study its ministry approach and became convinced that the cluster strategy was the way forward. Since its implementation the church has completely shifted its structure and operation to a cluster multiplication strategy. The church is now viewed as a hub, a central support for the clusters in its constellation, much like the Sheffield model. Sunday services are still offered each week, with about two-thirds of the people attending being cluster members.

Today about twenty clusters (that is the term still used) engage around five hundred people. The clusters involve between fifteen and forty people; once a cluster reaches forty participants it has to split. The clusters come in two types. The majority of the clusters are of the "modal" variety. They tend to be attractional in their methodology, gathering people together to experience Christian community. The second variety of cluster is the "sodal" type, which sees itself as mission based, composed of a group of missionaries who strategize together on how to evangelize a target population. Sodal cluster members literally move into a geographical area to center their lives in that neighborhood.

This is exactly what Andersen did with his family. He moved into an apartment complex with the idea of being a missionary to that community. Several other families also moved into the same complex to join in this mission. A total of seven apartment residents are now part of his cluster, with twenty mostly young adults plus kids. About ten to fifteen non-Christians are also "hanging around," even participating in church gatherings. Sune is not the leader of the cluster, but like all other staff leaders, is expected to be part of a cluster.

The cluster meets five times a month. On the first Sunday they do a community service project of some kind; then they invite people to a soup or supper gathering. Other meetings in the month are on Thursdays, with one given completely over to prayer. A second gathering is just the core community itself eating together, worshiping, vacuuming, doing dishes, hanging out for the evening, and helping each other with whatever needs doing. The third Thursday is a social night when they do something fun together, like going to the movies. Others are invited to this. A fourth Thursday is given to huddle groups of three to ten, with the focus on scripture reflection (what is God saying?) and life debriefing.

Sune's cluster is fairly typical, though there is a lot of flexibility from group to group. "We don't engineer anything," he says. Some other clusters have cell groups (two to three people) especially if the cluster is more spread out and does not meet every week However, all clusters have some shared practice. The up-in-out ministry dimensions are considered core DNA, though how this takes shape in each cluster is determined by that group of people. And, every cluster is expected to reproduce.

A person wanting to start a cluster is generally given permission, but the one requirement is that leaders will be in a huddle with other cluster leaders. The church has a highly developed leadership pipeline, focusing on raising leaders for every level of responsibility—there are strategies for training L10 leaders (leaders of 10), L50, L100, and L500 leaders. About eighty people are currently in cluster leader or cluster leader apprentice training.

Andersen admits to some struggles over the past seven years of implementing the cluster model of church. "Every initial cluster failed," he says. "It has taken three to four generations of clusters for us to get good at it." The church is now at the point where it can take on "must-win battles." The first "must-win" is a 2012 goal of having 20 percent of members to have come to faith in Christ outside of their home upbringing. Most of the growth of the church has been from people who were dechurched and are coming back into the church, which is a great win, but penetrating the larger culture will only happen with this "must-win" development. A second "must-win" for the church is to start twenty-five missional community plants or churches outside Aarhus over the next three years, creating a network of churches pursuing a cluster strategy in the four largest cities in Denmark.

The British Are Coming

Mike Breen has relocated to South Carolina to train church leaders in missional community strategy in the United States (www.3dministries.com). Dozens of church leaders are part of 3DM leadership communities of churches and are figuring out how to foster this movement across the United States.

Using missional communities as a church-planting strategy is not just isolated to the ECPN network. It is beginning to be adopted by some denominations in Britain. The Church of England and the Methodists have cooperated over the past five years in developing *Fresh Expressions*, an initiative to plant organic churches into people groups. Using the term *mixed economy of church*, they uphold traditional church while exploring a church that is "very different from church as we are used to it in the U.K." (*Fresh Expressions: An Introduction*, http://bit.ly/eNb9Oa). These initiatives reflect the core convictions of a missional community theology: that the gospel creates community and must be lived out in community with those it is trying to reach.

The missional community phenomenon in Europe is washing up on American shores. At least one denomination in the United States, the Baptist General Association of Virginia, has formed a partnership with Fresh Expressions to explore planting missional communities in this country as part of its denominational church-planting strategy.

The story of missional communities in Europe is not included in this book's anthology to demonstrate a causal connection. In fact, there isn't one—and that's part of the storyline. What we find is that people are coming up with similar ideas without ever having had conversation with each other. That's one sign of a spiritual movement. The Spirit seems to be inspiring a lot of similar thoughts among church leaders in Western cultures who share the common challenge of facing a post-congregational future. (I could just as easily have chosen to explore the missional community expression now under way in Australia!)

The other reason Europe gets a chapter in a book about the American church is to inspire hope. The emergence of missional communities in Europe signals the viability of this new church life form in decidedly post-congregational environments. That reality alone should have us American church leaders leaning in to take a closer look.

Some Americans are doing more than looking. They are already experimenting with this new church life form. Their stories begin right after a page turn.

4

SOMA COMMUNITIES

MISSIONAL COMMUNITIES
AS ORGANIZING
ARCHITECTURE

Before teaming up to launch Soma Communities, Jeff Vander-stelt and Caesar Kalinowski spent years leading in large, more traditional church models. They had become friends, often wondering together about how different most Christians' lives are from what they read in scripture.

Jeff and Caesar came to several conclusions that continue to inform and guide their ministry. One was that the Bible is the story of God's people, a people who were and are both "called" and "sent" to express through actions and words the good news of Jesus. They also became convinced that the gospel involves more than personal salvation. The good news is that God wants to bring restoration to all things, meaning the gospel has implications for communities as well as individuals, for societal issues as well as individual relationships. Further, the gospel needs to be lived out in God's people, to be incarnated in the lives of people who identify themselves with his mission. But sadly, these two church leaders surmised, most Christians don't know how to live their lives ordered around the good news so that they make a difference in the world around them. They need help to do this, specifically, the support of a like-minded community.

Feeling that God was up to something new, Jeff and Caesar decided to put their convictions into practice. Jeff and Jayne Vanderstelt first moved back to Seattle in 2002 to be a part of a new church plant led by Bill Clem called *Doxa* in West Seattle. From there, that church sent them out to plant in Tacoma. Caesar and Tina Kalinowski moved out from Chicago shortly thereafter to join them and a small core of people.

As Caesar tells it, "We began as a small group of people asking the questions, 'What does the good news of Jesus Christ look like to the people we live with and love?' and 'How should we live so they can also experience God's love?'" Jeff and Caesar kept those two questions uppermost on their minds as they explored a different way to be church. Addressing those two questions led the Soma team to create their distinctive approach to missional communities. The leaders wanted Soma to grow out of believers' strong identity of being the people of God, not just as a result of doing a bunch of church programming. This led to the decision to not launch a worship service but instead to launch missional communities.

After a year of praying and preparing, the first four missional communities were established in various neighborhoods on September 14, 2004. From this start of four communities with several dozen people, Soma Communities is now approaching a hundred missional groups composed of over a thousand people, with thousands more served through their ministry.

Missional Community Definitions

Soma is very clear that they do not consider missional communities to be small groups, Bible studies, support groups, social activist groups, or weekly meetings. They declare that "a missional community consists of a committed core of believers (*family*) who live out the mission together (*missionaries*) in a specific area or to a particular people group by demonstrating the gospel in tangible forms (*servants*) and declaring the gospel to others—both those who believe it and those who are being exposed to it (*learners*)."

As Caesar puts it, "We wanted to make sure our *doing* comes out of our *being*." This requires that people understand that missional community rests on a proper grasp of the gospel, along with its implications for a believer's identity in Christ and how the gospel can be lived out in basic life rhythms.

The Gospel

Soma teaches that the gospel is "the good news that God has come to rescue and renew creation in and through the work of Jesus Christ." They believe it must be understood in two perspectives.

The first is a thematic approach, getting the theological basics right. The gospel is the power of God for salvation to everyone who believes. Human beings are sinful because we choose to live life for us, our way, and not for God, his way. Sin is so pervasive it destructively affects our relationships with God, others, ourselves, and the rest of creation. God has chosen to rescue us from the power and penalty of sin through the redemptive work of Jesus. When we repent and receive this gift of salvation we are saved from the penalty of sin and receive the Spirit's power to help us overcome sin.

We must also come to understand the gospel as a story, where we see the *purpose* of God in saving us. That purpose is the restoration of all things destroyed by sin. In other words, the gospel isn't just about our individual happiness or

God's plan for *my* life; it is about God's plan *for the world*. Eventually the whole world will be renewed. This takes place as the disciples of Jesus make other disciples who live out their role as agents of renewal in all areas of culture—the arts, business, politics, families, education—all domains of human activity.

This, then, is what it means to live missionally—joining God in his restorative work. The people of God actually become an alternative city within a city to display, as a foretaste, what the eternal city will be like. The Soma teaching on the gospel sums it up this way: "When we repent of our sin and receive the new life that Jesus has offered us, we begin a journey of restoration inside and out. And not just for us—but for the entire world!"

Identity—Who We Are

The definition of missional community builds on our identity, expressed in four primary ways. We are children of God who live and care for each other as a *family*. God has always desired a people who would live in such a way that the world would know what he is like. This initial expression in the garden is reemphasized in the call of Abraham's family and eventually extended in the New Testament to all followers of Jesus, who acknowledge God as Father and live in his ways. As family we have the obligation to care for one another—both physically and spiritually. This gains expression in the covenant life we live together in community.

As followers of Jesus we are also *missionaries*. This means we are sent by God to restore all things to himself. This sending was modeled for us in the life and mission of Jesus, who now likewise sends us into the world to live in such a way that people can see and experience what God is truly like. We live this out as a missional community.

We are also *servants* who serve others as a way of life. Again, Jesus demonstrated what this kind of life looks like. Basically it means we do *whatever* needs doing *whenever* it's needed and *wherever* it leads us (Soma labels this teaching W3). The missional community becomes a delivery system for this service as well as providing accountability to encourage this way of life.

Finally we are *learners*, disciples of Jesus who take responsibility for our own development and that of others. Even the Son of God lived life as a learner. In his early years he learned from family, religious teachers, his village, as well as from his Father. He created a band of learners (disciples) in order to establish his movement. Today we are still being called as followers, meaning we adopt a life of learning and, like the early disciples, help others in their own development. Again, the missional community provides us with the opportunity to do both of these.

To help all missional community participants integrate these dimensions of their identity, Soma has developed an online discipleship assessment tool called MRI that poses 140 questions in twelve categories. Caesar explains, "This self-scored assessment informs where a person is at in their discipleship maturity, looking not just at 'head knowledge,' but at the 'head, heart, and hands' of the participants—what they know, how it has begun to shape their hearts and motives, and whether they are actually living differently in light of this truth." Resources for each person's further development are made available online.

Life Rhythms—How We Live

Six daily, cultural rhythms give guidance to Soma missional communities in terms of what they do together. Each missional community assesses exactly how these rhythms play out in their setting.

Story-formed: We Understand, Experience, and Intersect with God's Story and Others'

We are all intersecting God's Story, which he has been unfolding since before time began. Interacting with God's Word from this perspective allows us to understand it and figure out how our lives are shaped by it so we can engage it more intentionally.

Each year the Soma missional communities go through ten weeks of reacquainting themselves with God's Story—the big picture—and engage the Bible throughout the rest of the year through this lens. Soma has developed a unique discipleship set of biblical narratives called the Story-formed Way. Community leaders are specifically trained on how to lead the community through this dialogical form of teaching. Coming at scripture through this perspective keeps the focus on each person's figuring out what God is revealing to him or her about his or her life. Caesar observes: "This approach eliminates the need for 'experts' to 'explain the meaning of the text' while everyone else listens. The Story-formed Way of learning allows for newcomers to be as engaged as existing members of the community because the focus of the dialogue is on insights related to the story of the day.

Listen: We Set Aside Regular Times to Listen to God Both "Backward" and "Forward"

Jesus provides the example here by routinely practicing this approach in his own prayer life in order to know the Father's will. Engagement with God's Word—the Story and the Son—helps us to listen "backward" while the Spirit helps us listen "forward" to hear what God is saying to us today. This is why Bible engagement and prayer practice are important routines of each community.

Celebrate: We Gather Together to Celebrate God's Extravagant Blessings

The point of gathering is to celebrate all that God is doing in and among the people of the missional community. These gatherings happen weekly at the community level but also at the "larger family" level of Expressions (clusters of missional communities)—in Sunday gatherings, which are held at multiple locations in the Seattle-Tacoma area. Participation in the larger gatherings is less frequent than those at the home base of the missional community. The larger gatherings also provide some attractional element to the Soma strategy, particularly in introducing the missional community concept to already-churched people and helping to guide them into a community expression that is appropriate for them.

Bless: We Intentionally Bless Others Through Words, Gifts, or Actions

God created a people to bless the nations (Genesis 12:1–3). He came himself to bless all people in Jesus. Now, as members of his *soma* (Greek for *body*), this same mission is lived out in us as we bless others. Part of every missional community agenda is the decision about who the community will bless and make disciples among as part of their life together in corporate service. For instance, the community may choose to adopt a neighborhood school as their common mission. But each person in the community is also expected personally to intentionally and tangibly bless people each week as part of living on mission.

Eat: We Regularly Eat Meals with Others to Invite Them into the Community of God

It is no accident that Jesus called us to remember him and his sacrifice for us through a meal. Meals are daily reminders of our need for God's provision and his physical and spiritual blessings. Eating with others becomes an important rhythm for remembering this truth. Missional community members are encouraged to and accountable for eating meals with people not in their immediate family or close friends on a regular basis.

Re-create: We Take Time to Rest, Play, Create, and Restore Beauty in Ways That Reflect God to Others

Soma missional communities play together and party together. This time is as significant as any other in honoring the biblical idea of rest. They use this as a way of inviting others into relationship with them and God. They also figure out ways to add beauty to their surroundings, whether in beautification projects or art projects in local neighborhoods.

Each community determines how it will weave these six rhythms into their life together. To do so is a key part of the covenanting process as missional communities pledge their lives to each other. The missional community also helps each individual participant figure out how these rhythms can be expressed in their personal identities as missionaries, servants, and learners.

DNA Groups—Getting It Up Close and Personal

Because life change occurs most often in the context of supportive relationships, Soma missional communities have a microchurch component to provide this significant element.

These are called *DNA* (discipleship, nurture, accountability) *groups*. They typically consist of three people—men with men, women with women—who meet together weekly to encourage each other to grow in and live out their gospel identity and gospel rhythm.

Each DNA group decides its own meeting time and place. The encounters ideally involve each of the components of discipleship, nurture, and accountability. The groups get into each other's lives by asking lots of debriefing questions: *How are you doing? Who are you loving well or not so well? What fears are you living with? How are you obeying Jesus? How are you doing on the goals you have set?* Of course, praying for one another plays a big part of these connections when the DNA group meets and as they support each other all week.

DNA groups are formed generally one of two ways. Some people put their own group together with friends. Others ask their missional community leader or elder to help them find a DNA group that fits them. Helping people create this kind of life support is a critical role of missional community leaders.

Expressions

Missional communities grow and multiply (their size ranges from eight to twenty people, with twelve to fourteen being typical). The goal is for each missional community to multiply within twelve months. From the initial four missional communities almost one hundred communities have developed with over one thousand people currently connected to them.

When a group of missional communities who live in close proximity to each other begin to work together to uniquely express the gospel in their area, they form what is called an *Expression*. An Expression is led by the leaders from the constituent missional communities under the authority of a local Soma elder. Expressions gather together at different times and in different ways for equipping, worship, training, and to jointly serve in their area. Caesar explains, "Each Expression portrays what it means to be church a little differently, in ways that are unique to it."

Soma Life—An Example

Let's see how missional community architecture plays out in real life. Each missional community leader develops a group covenant that each member signs. The group covenant is framed around the gospel identity and gospel rhythms that are part of the Soma culture. Here are some excerpts from the covenant that the Grant Park missional community developed for a recent year.

Gospel Identity

I believe that I have been given a new identity in Christ because of the gospel. I am a part of God's family on mission sent to serve our world and continually learn to walk in his ways.

Missionaries
We believe we are sent to:

• People in Grant Park

Writer's note: Missional communities tend to be geographically located and neighborhood-centric. Some families, sensing a call to serve a particular part of the city, have sold homes and relocated from one part of Tacoma to another to be part of a specific missional community. Commenting on this phenomenon, Caesar observes: "This is what missionaries do—they move to live among the people group they are called to serve."

- Parents and teachers of Edison Elementary

Writer's note: Each missional community identifies key people groups they want to bless. These can be people groups (such as an immigrant population or people who work in a certain industry or live in a certain neighborhood). They can also be schools, community agencies, or some other organization that taps into the passion of the missional community. The Grant Park missional community has chosen the parents and teachers of Edison Park Elementary, a local school in the neighborhood. Other communities have covenanted around a variety of other people groups. A sample of these include single moms and their kids in their neighborhood, youth at a high school, kids at a middle school, business owners in a particular business district, military personnel and their families, a group of twenty-somethings that frequent the clubs in a certain part of town, and young people caught up in the illegal sex trade industry. The list is as long and as varied as the number of missional communities.

Servants
We are committed to serve by cleaning up the Grant Park neighborhood, caring for children after school, volunteering at Edison Elementary, fixing Edith's home, and developing a neighborhood care and watch group.

Learners
We will devote ourselves to working through an assessment to determine equipping needs for those in our missional community, being trained in basic discipleship so that we

can train others, and sharing the gospel verbally with Grant Park and parents and teachers of Edison Elementary, reading through the Bible.

Family
We will speak the truth in love and submit to one another in this, refrain from gossip or slander and be reconciled when we do, forgive one another, pray for one another, bear with one another, and meet together regularly.

Gospel Rhythms

Gospel rhythms help explain how missional communities live out the gospel together.

Story-formed
We will learn and communicate the Story of God together and become familiar with each other's personal stories and the stories of the people in Grant Park and the parents and teachers of Edison Elementary.

Listen
We will listen to God together when we gather, regularly set aside times personally to listen to God, listen to God while listening to those in our missional community and mission, identify those who listen to God well, and seek out more training.

Celebrate
We will gather regularly with our Expression and missional community to celebrate God's grace, come together to celebrate special events, join in the celebrations in Grant Park and at Edison in ways that intentionally demonstrate the gospel, and create or serve at four key celebrations annually within our community.

Bless

Together we will make an inventory of what we have been given for the sake of blessing others, make our blessings known to Grant Park and Edison so they can gain access to what we have, grow in our financial giving together by 1 percent this year, and transform Edith's backyard.

Eat

We will break bread together weekly in homes remembering Jesus's death, eat a weekly meal together, have one open meal monthly to invite people into our community, and pick one restaurant in the central district to eat at regularly (at least twice a month).

Re-create

We will work with the city to remodel Jefferson Park, take a vacation together by the end of next summer, and start a gardener's club for Grant Park.

Soma Communities Leadership

One can argue that a network church of missional communities requires a greater leadership focus than traditional, hierarchical models of congregation. Leadership must be cultivated in each facet of community life.

Triperspectivalism

A leadership philosophy called *triperspectivalism* undergirds the Soma approach to leadership recruitment, deployment, and development.

Triperspectivalism is a shared leadership approach based on the elements of prophet, priest, and king as related in the scriptures. The prophetic type of leader focuses on normative standards—the unchanging truths of God's character, the gospel message, and the mission of the church. The prophet is always calling God's people to faithfulness and to align life with his truth. The priestly type of leader concentrates on the care of the soul. Their focus will be to make sure that people are caring for one another and that the needs of the community are met. The kingly leader pays attention to structures and systems, strategic thinking, day-to-day governing, and the oversight necessary to support the mission. Kingly leadership is not exercised in a "lording over" manner, but as a servant.

All three leadership styles need to be present at every level of the church. Soma Communities in Tacoma is headed by three leaders who demonstrate these roles. Jeff Vanderstelt (prophet), Abe Meysenburg (priest), and Caesar Kalinowski (king) form the nucleus of a team of elders who oversee Soma. They are each accountable to each other overall in character, but specifically charged to serve the family in their area of competence and call. Each missional community has identified a similar leadership tripod. Every person who feels inclined to form a missional community is instructed to begin by building a shared-leadership team with these three perspectives in place.

Leadership Development and Responsibilities

People who feel called to lead a missional community commit to several levels of preparation and accountability. Besides covenanting to maintain their own personal spiritual disciplines of prayer and Bible study, they also promise to participate in 80 percent of monthly leaders' meetings and attend the Soma school (an immersionist experience designed to train missional community leaders) either before they begin their leadership or within the first twelve months. Each leader meets monthly with his or her elder coach and undergoes evaluation throughout the year.

Leadership expectations and demands are substantive and specific. Missional community leaders are trained to identify coleaders for their own communities as well as discover and develop leaders for multiplying communities. They lead by example in having two to three relationships with not-yet-believers whom they are intentionally discipling to Jesus. They help each person in their missional community develop an intentional life plan based on the Soma MRI assessment and their personal goals. Leaders check in with each person monthly as well as foster communication between community members each week. They are committed to praying for each person in their missional community on a weekly basis. In addition, they review DNA progress on a quarterly basis, making sure that people are participating and growing. Each year the missional community leader leads the group through the Story-formed Way and the gospel-centered finance and budgeting class.

Some sample questions that each leader works through in the monthly session with an elder or coach are as follows:

Is my love for the Word growing?

Am I growing in my ability to clearly articulate the gospel in any setting?

Do I live with the confidence that God is great so I don't have to be in control?

Do I live with the confidence that God is glorious so I don't have to fear others?

Do I live with the confidence that God is good so I don't have to look elsewhere?

Do I live with the confidence that God is gracious so I don't have to prove myself? (These last four questions are what Soma leaders refer to as the 4 Gs, adopted from author Tim Chester.)

If married, have I had regular date nights with my wife?

If a parent, how am I doing at leading my kids spiritually?

The development of missional community leaders matches their leadership challenges, focusing on their character, capacity, and competence.

A Month in the Life of a Soma Community Leader

Todd and Hannah Morr moved to the South End of Tacoma about three years ago. They have four kids between the ages of one year and eight years old. Hannah is a stay-at-home mom. The Morrs lead a missional community that includes four other young couples that have eight more kids among them—with eleven of the twelve children under eight years of age. This is their third missional community, having multiplied twice from their original group. This current missional community has been together a little over a year, with plans to multiply sometime in 2011. Together with six other missional communities, they form the South End Expression.

Here are Todd's diary notes from a recent month's engagement as a missional community leader.

Week 1

Monday: (day) Hannah organizes a play date with some MC moms and some non-Christian neighbor moms. **(night)** Todd plays basketball with guys from South End Expression and a non-Christian friend.

Wednesday: MC has a meal together, catches up on each other's lives, and discusses one of the 4 Gs (God is great, good, gracious, and glorious).

Thursday: Todd meets with his DNA while Hannah watches the kids.

Friday: Todd and Hannah have non-Christian friends over (who have two kids) to grill and hang out.

Saturday: Todd mows the grass of the single mom next door (along with mowing his own grass).

Sunday: Todd and Hannah participate in the Sunday morning gathering and sit with others from their MC.

Week 2

Monday: **(day)** Hannah organizes a play date with some MC moms and some non-Christian neighbor moms. **(night)** Todd and Hannah and some others from their MC join members of the South End Expression to help host a meal and life skills evening for homeless families and single moms connected with two partner organizations of Soma.

Tuesday: Hannah takes extra cookies she has baked to non-Christian neighbors next door.

Wednesday: MC has meal together, catches up on each other's lives, and discusses one of the 4 Gs. They finish with prayer and some discussion about future opportunities to influence neighbors.

Thursday: Hannah meets with her DNA while Todd watches the kids.

Saturday: **(day)** Todd and Hannah buy and drop off groceries for one of the two single moms that their MC has "adopted." **(night)** Todd and Hannah invite non-Christian neighbors over for dessert and yard games (bean bag toss).

Sunday: **(day)** Todd and Hannah participate in the Sunday morning gathering and sit with others from their MC. **(night)**

Todd and Hannah participate in monthly training for MC leaders with all of the Soma MC leaders.

Week 3

Monday: (day) Hannah organizes two weeks' worth of meals for a non-Christian mom who has just had a baby. Other women from the MC and from the South End Expression help in preparing and delivering the meals. **(night)** Todd plays basketball with guys from South End Expression and a non-Christian friend.

Wednesday: MC has a meal together, catches up on each other's lives, and discusses one of the 4 Gs. They finish with prayer and share some stories about recent opportunities they have all had to speak with and influence their non-Christian neighbors.

Thursday: Todd meets with his DNA while Hannah watches the kids.

Friday: Todd and Hannah meet with a couple in their MC who are having marital problems.

Saturday: Todd and Hannah go for a walk at the waterfront with their kids and their non-Christian friends and their kids. Todd mows the grass of the single mom next-door along with mowing his own yard.

Sunday: Todd and Hannah participate in the Sunday morning gathering and sit with others from their MC.

Week 4

Monday: Hannah organizes a play date with some MC moms and some non-Christian neighbor moms.

Wednesday: MC has meal together, catches up on each other's lives, and discusses one of the 4 Gs. They finish with prayer and discussion about future opportunities to influence their neighbors

Thursday: Hannah meets with her DNA while Todd watches the kids.

Friday: Todd and Hannah have non-Christian friends over to grill and play with their kids on the trampoline.

Saturday: Guys from the MC go hiking together.

Sunday: (day) Todd and Hannah participate in the Sunday morning gathering and sit with others from their MC. **(night)** Todd and Hannah meet with the other leaders from the Sound End Expression to further discuss the training that was presented in week 2.

Todd admits that trying to balance the demands of living out the biblical identities of family, missionary, servant, and learner along with the demands of working, parenting their four small children, loving each other as spouses, discipling the MC, and demonstrating and proclaiming the gospel to neighbors can be "a very tiring and demanding way to live." But, he adds, "very, very rich at the same time!"

Commenting on Todd's diary, Caesar noted that "three or four other couples and their kids in Todd's missional community would have similar experiences this month to share." This comment highlights the incredible intentionality of Soma missional community life. Church is not an add-on element to the rest of life; it is a *way of life*. The missional communities of Soma are living as missionaries in the largely non-Christian population of the Pacific Northwest. Many of these activities are usual things in anyone's life but done differently by people who see and live life as a mission trip.

What's Next?

Part of the short history of Soma includes other churches joining with them (*Pneuma, The Sound, Harambee*) to create a growing church with many different forms and locations through the South Puget Sound. Soma missional communities now meet for gatherings in three locations on Sunday (two in Tacoma and one in Renton) and in missional communities all over the area throughout the week.

Soma Communities currently offers its Soma School weeklong experience for those who are interested in the missional community concept. As a result they have trained church leaders from all over the world. Soma leaders want to become more intentional in helping to seed a network of these types of churches. Consequently they are in the early phases of determining if and how they could resource the development of Soma Communities in ten target cities in the western part of the United States. Work has begun and Soma Communities has been established in Portland, San Francisco, Los Angeles, San Diego, Boise, and Phoenix.

Soma Communities provides an example of a network church that is composed of missional communities as its organizing principle. Although highly structured in its methodology and leadership, it is also highly contextualized and organic in its basic component—the missional community.

5

CAMPUS
RENEWAL UT

MISSIONAL COMMUNITIES AS
CAMPUS EVANGELISM STRATEGY

In fall 1991 Justin Christopher matriculated into the freshman class at the University of Texas at Austin (UT). He had become a Jesus follower three years earlier as a high school student through the ministry of Student Venture, the high school ministry of Campus Crusade for Christ. Within a year of his conversion he had been gripped by a vision of revival on his high school campus. He started a weekly "pancakes and prayer" gathering and actively began to share his faith with other classmates. When several football players responded by becoming Jesus followers Justin began to disciple them in a Bible study in his home. He considered these activities and results to be "normative" for campus life, a conviction he brought with him to UT.

Soon after arriving in Austin Justin gathered up a group of friends and began praying daily for revival at the university. They met each morning at seven o'clock. During the second week, another group called up to say they had been doing the same thing—praying each morning for a campus revival. The two groups joined forces and became the core group of a prayer team that Justin prayed with every day during his four years as a student at UT.

What started as a prayer group grew into a prayer movement. Beginning the first semester of Justin's sophomore year (1992) the prayer effort expanded to include students from about twenty of the thirty campus ministries that were operating at the time. This group gathered every Friday afternoon to share a story or two of what God was doing and read and pray through scripture. In spring 1993 the first concert of prayer was conducted, with several hundred people turning out to spend the night in prayer. This became a part of every semester afterward.

A watershed event in Justin's senior year changed his life's trajectory. Called Rez Week (short for Resurrection Week), it was a week of prayer, worship, outreach, and fellowship around Easter involving a united effort of many campus ministries. The week saw lots of students' making decisions to become Jesus followers but it also did something else. It convinced Justin and others that the Body of Christ could work as one to see the University of Texas transformed by the gospel. This realization was so profound that Justin found himself wondering, "Could this be a calling for me?" After taking a year off after graduation to raise support, Justin returned to the UT campus to pursue the vision of campus renewal.

Fifteen Years Later

Fast-forward to 2010. Justin is still at UT, still raising support for his ministry, and seeing signs of real progress in the transformation of college students and the campus. So why am I telling his story?

My interest in Justin's ministry centers on the development of missional communities as an evangelism strategy to reach the college campus, a notoriously challenging mission field in North America. Missional communities are one of four components of a five-part strategy for Campus Renewal Ministries (CRM)—an organization operating now on several college campuses around the country. The other four pieces of strategy include prayer mobilization of students, catalytic events, spiritual mapping (collecting data on the spiritual condition of students and student ministries), and fusion (the weekly gathering of campus ministry directors for prayer and relationship building). Although each part of the strategy has its unique contribution, it was the creation of missional communities in 2004 that exploded the impact of college ministry on the UT campus, particularly with regard to evangelism.

The decision to begin missional communities was prompted by the discoveries uncovered through a "spiritual mapping" process in 2002. The results were sobering. Only three hundred students a year were becoming Jesus followers on campus through the efforts of several dozen campus ministries, some of which saw not a single convert in a year's time. Of the students in the various campus ministries 89 percent were Jesus followers before coming to UT (57 percent had made this decision as a child; 32 percent in junior high or senior high school). The campus Christians were bubbled off—60 percent of them did not have any unbelieving friends and only 26 percent had spiritual conversations with their nonbelieving friends more than once a month. In light of these realities, Justin concluded: "The fact was that we were not reaching unbelieving students with the gospel of Jesus. For the most part, we were just building a community for the Christian students that came to UT." (Justin chronicles the UT story in his book *Campus Renewal* [Campus Renewal Ministries, 2010]. The book speaks in depth about all five of the campus renewal strategies.)

The leaders of the Christian ministries on campus came to the conclusion that remedying this situation would require a change in thinking, in structures, and in programming. The change in thinking can be described mainly as shifting from a ministry strategy aimed at Christians ("come to") into a missionary strategy aimed at unbelievers ("go to"). This required looking at the UT campus as a mission field composed of many different people groups or cultures (dorms, Greek houses, sports teams, academic departments, ethnic student organizations, social clubs, and so on). For 2010, CRM estimates that there are over 550 people groups at the University of Texas, with an average of fifty students per community. Connecting with these people groups would require creating an incarnational presence of campus missionaries in missional communities embedded within these largely unreached people groups. College students were going to have to become front-line missionaries, not consumers of college ministry programming.

This change in perspective called for a shift in ministry structure from one that mostly supported weekly gatherings of believers into one focused on the recruitment, deployment, and training of missional communities led by college students. Staffing and resources had to be redirected to this strategy instead of focusing on creating more events and typical college ministry initiatives.

The result of shifting to a missional community strategy has been pretty amazing. Twenty missional communities were launched in 2004. That number has risen tenfold to 220 missional communities in 2010. The number of students becoming followers of Jesus climbed to 625 the same year, a direct correlation to the employment of a missional community strategy. In addition to the experience students enjoy while at UT, being part of a missional community trains them in how to go out into the world with the mentality of a missionary. In this way, the campus renewal efforts at UT are not only touching the campus in Austin, but also preparing this generation of missional college leaders to touch the world.

Missional Communities Take Off

The strategic switch to a missional community approach gained acceleration through several key developments in quick succession. In 2002 the campus ministers of the various ministries made the commitment to "campus saturation through missional communities." In 2003 the strategy gained traction through the introduction of intentional training for students on how to live like missionaries on campus. This material, called the Retrospect Course, was adapted from the training material that Glenn Smith had developed for New Church Initiatives, basically wedding church-planting insights with college ministry outreach. Within three years most college ministries (for example, Hyde Park Baptist, First Evangelical Free Church, and the Texas Wesley United Methodist Campus Ministry) had customized this training for their own students. Two local congregations with significant college ministries, the Austin Stone Community Church and Hill Country Bible Church UT, also switched to the missional community strategy (the Austin Stone story is part of the next chapter).

The shared strategy of launching missional communities by the various campus ministries has also created an environment of cooperation and collaboration rather than a spirit of competition. In 2009, ten ministries at UT formed a partnership called Renovate UT. The ministry leaders meet monthly to report on their missional communities and hold a united celebration once a semester. They also share a database of all their missional community leaders so that the campus ministry directors can know who is doing what, where, and with whom. This shared information allows for leaders to connect students across ministry lines. This has resulted in the dramatic increase of the number of missional communities at UT over the past few years.

Spark Groups

In 2009 CRM decided to produce a training curriculum for missional communities—called *Spark Groups*—that all ministries could use. It pulled together the insights from the missional community experiences over the years and added the equipping components of several campus ministries.

The Spark Course is taught in person by CRM staff as well as online at www.campusrenewal.org. This training plays a key role in helping shift the mind-set of students from seeing college ministry as a retreat into seeing it as missional living. The "Eight Spark Group Practices" (outlined in *Campus Renewal*, pp. 157–158) is taught in an eight-week course, typically done in small groups around meals. Looking at these eight practices gives us a good window into how these missional communities develop and function. Remember that college students comprise and lead these missional communities. Spark Group training is for all group participants.

1. **Pick a people group.** *Discern what people group God is calling to be your mission field.* As already mentioned CRM has identified more than 550 people groups. The latest edition of *The Longhorn Chronicles*, CRM's annual publication of its

current spiritual mapping surveys, lists the following people groups:

- Twenty-five dorms with more than one hundred dorm floors, ten co-ops, and fifty student apartments
- About sixty fraternities and sororities
- About two dozen varsity sports and forty club sports
- About one hundred ethnic groups and ethnic student organizations
- Almost one thousand registered student organizations and interest groups
- About seventeen colleges, seventy-one majors, and one hundred academic student organizations

2. **Partner with other believers.** *Ask other believers to join you in a mission.* Missional communities may involve students from different ministries who live in the same place, attend the same classes, participate in the same activities, and feel called to the same people group. This is very much like building the core group for a church launch. Expectations need to be clearly established. Inviting other students to be a part of a Spark Group involves opening up to them about the calling to be a missionary, not just inviting them to join you in being nice to people you want to touch.

3. **Pray and plan.** *Pray every week and ask the Lord to reveal his plans for you.* The weekly gathering of the Spark Group involves prayer for each other, for the campus, for lost friends, as well as to give praise to God for what he is doing. The key assumption is that prayer helps our hearts be captured by God's heart. God is at work in the people around us; prayer helps us get in touch with his engagement with them. It also amps up our compassion for those in our community.

4. **Presence** in the community. *Spend a significant amount of time each week in your community building relationships with many people.* Early on, directors of campus ministries moving to the missional community strategy realized that collegiate ministries were often gobbling up all the time that college students had for relationships. This meant that the involvement in campus ministry frequently resulted in no time left for building friendships with people who are unbelievers. Programming had to be simplified and streamlined in order to release students into being missionaries, giving them time to cultivate their mission field.

The goal is for students to spend ten hours per week with their missional community. Spark Groups figure out how students in their target people group spend their time and how they can join them. This time commitment requires a great deal of intentionality as well as some creativity. Time can be spent studying together in recreation (sports, Internet, video games), working, or just hanging out.

5. **Prepare** the way for the gospel. *Demonstrate the gospel to your community by being loving, living a holy life, and revealing the power of God.* Each part of that admonition is important. Spark Group participants strategize on how to demonstrate all three components.

Students can demonstrate *being loving* through service to members of their target people group as well as by organizing service projects that they can invite others to participate in. Hospitality also plays a big key to loving people and can be demonstrated as simply as keeping the dorm room door open most of the time or by inviting people over to watch TV or have dinner.

Living a holy life means figuring out what *not to do* as well as choosing what *to do*. The idea is to provoke interest by being different—in the world, but not of it. By practicing forgiveness and living selfless lives, being an encourager and living generously, Jesus followers *do* create an intrigue about what makes them tick. By not joining in gossip, practicing discipline in drinking, avoiding drugs, refusing to cheat or plagiarize, missional students stand out by what they *do not do*.

Students *reveal the power of God* by asking God to reveal himself to people in supernatural ways (their dreams, for instance). They can tell others they are praying for them—and then do it! Spark Group participants pray for the miraculous healing from sickness or addiction for their friends. They may ask for a remedy for depression, anxiety, or financial stress. As God answers these prayers the way is prepared for sharing the gospel.

6. **Proclaim** the gospel. *Initiate spiritual conversations by asking questions, sharing your story, and sharing the gospel.* Students need to ask God for opportunities to share their faith, but they also need to be ready when the time comes. Spark Group training helps students understand how asking good questions can open up conversations that can be spiritually charged. Knowing how to share one's story and how to listen to another's story is also an important competency in being a good missionary. Spark Group members specifically support these efforts each week through prayer and encouragement.

7. **Produce** disciples. *Make disciples by meeting weekly to study the Bible, teaching your friends to obey the commands of Jesus.* Spark Groups read whole books of the Bible or chunks of chapters, typically beginning with the gospels so they can focus on the teachings of Jesus. When they come together they ask questions of what the teaching is, what questions it raises for them, what the passage asks them to do. CRM calls this approach to scripture "obedience-based training." They then will indicate something they intend to do because of the teaching and offer to be willing to be held accountable for it

when they get together again. Often unbelievers are present and they need to feel free to ask questions in an environment that encourages exploration, not just coming up with the "right" answer.

Spark Groups are cautioned that they are not primarily a Bible study group. Although Bible study is an important part of group life, it is a *means* of discipleship, not an *end*. Other group practices of prayer, service, hospitality, and hanging out—these are all important.

8. **Reproduce** Spark Groups. *Plant more Spark Groups by reproducing leaders and sending them to more unreached people groups.* This part of the missional community strategy is highly affected by the college campus environment. Student populations turn over every four or five years, so it is important always to be raising up younger leaders who will be able to carry on the work when others graduate. In addition, students typically are part of multiple people groups, so they might begin to sense a call to begin a Spark Group with a community that is currently underserved by missional community engagement.

Leaders of Spark Groups meet throughout the semester for training and encouragement. The group I sat with on the Wednesday I visited had missional community leaders from the aerospace field, radio and television studies, the nursing school, liberal arts, and one leader wanting to start a missional community with Israeli students. Justin convened the group and conducted the session. Each leader was asked to share (what's going on), pray (for another leader's work), and celebrate (identify one "win" for the week). In similar settings other campus ministry leaders are pouring themselves into these students, who are learning to live like missionaries in their college setting.

The Longhorn Chronicles

Each fall CRM produces a kind of "state of the church" document for the UT campus, called *The Longhorn Chronicles*. The statistics are generated by surveys collected from the more than sixty campus ministries. The *Chronicles* are released at a five-hour meeting of all campus ministers and become the basis for strategy discussions that day and afterward. The report includes a wealth of information about the Christian community and ministry on campus, including the missional communities' development.

Here is a sampling of the information shared with the campus ministries in fall 2010, with emphasis on missional communities statistics:

- Of the roughly 51,000 students at UT Austin, 4,934 (9.7 percent) are involved in campus ministry. This is up from 6 percent in 2004.
- Missional communities numbered 218 (at least 58 in dormitories and student housing, 22 in the Greek system, 19 in varsity and club sports teams, 42 in colleges and academic clubs, 26 in clubs and interest groups, and 44 in ethnic groups).
- Missional communities in dorms, co-ops, and Greek houses have had success building meaningful relationships and leading friends to follow Jesus. Those in club, colleges, sports teams, and ethnic groups have struggled.
- Fifty percent of Christian students are part of an unbelieving community at UT.
- There were 2,168 unbelieving students in relationships with missional community leaders.
- There were 334 Christian students who led a friend to follow Jesus (5.5 percent of the Christian community).

- There were 1,321 Christian students who shared the gospel often (21.6 percent of the Christian community).
- There were 625 students who began to follow Jesus.
- More than sixty missional communities were identified to be started this year.

Contextualization

The development of missional communities at UT expresses a strategy to address a specific issue identified by campus ministers: the lack of penetration of Christian students into the larger campus population. The unique culture of college typically affords only a few years of engagement at a critical time in students' personal and spiritual formation. This context heavily influences the expression of missional community at UT, which is defined as "a community of Christ followers, on mission with God in obedience to the Holy Spirit that demonstrates and declares the Gospel of Jesus Christ to a specific people group."

The missional community experience for these college students is not designed to be the primary church experience for the participants. The students involved in missional communities typically attend some church gathering on weekends and even participate in campus ministry activities apart from their missional community engagement. Students who become followers of Jesus are encouraged to integrate into some local congregation on campus or in the city.

The Longhorn Chronicles—Personal Edition

Four stories of current missional communities, in the voice of the students, give us a flavor of the energy and character of the experience.

Jenny Dietz is an honors history major, planning on graduating in December 2012. Here is part of her missional community story.

The Liberal Arts Honors (LAH) missional community started when a friend and I decided to get together to pray for our small portion of the College of Liberal Arts. We told a few other friends about our weekly prayer hour at the Campus House of Prayer, they told a few more friends, and soon we had a group. From that first week on we have continued to meet weekly in a time of prayer and accountability. Each week our members tell the group one concrete thing that he or she is going to do to reach the lost in LAH. Whether it's going on a lunch date with another student, studying in the LAH commons area, attending a LAH social event, or just a friendly Facebook message to keep in touch, our community members are pushed to actively be missional every week of the school year.

Though our missional community has been around for less than two semesters, God has worked through us in wonderful ways. Initially, only a few of our core group members were willing to openly share the gospel. UT can be intimidating!

As those few shared their stories with the others, the entire group was encouraged, freed from the fear of man, and filled with a spirit of boldness. Dozens of students have heard the gospel from the lips of our missional community members and we have seen two students put their faith in Jesus! Both of those salvations were the result of the development of a deep, trusting friendship. We strongly value the relationships that we build with nonbelievers in our community; they are not projects, challenges, or tasks to complete. They are people whom we love and we love them so much that we can't bear the idea of them living without the hope offered by the Cross. The missional community members who led those students to Christ are discipling them and encouraging them to share their faith with others.

Peter Schulte reflects on why missional communities are an important strategy for reaching people right where they already are.

During my second year at UT I lived in San Jacinto Dorm and my roommate, whom I knew through campus ministry, was an RA (resident assistant). We held a Bible study in the dorm every week, mostly made up of guys who we were pouring into and challenging to live on mission to reach their friends. There were a few lost students in the dorm who were interested enough to come to our Bible study sometimes, but they generally didn't feel comfortable there. Our missional community focused on just spending time hanging out with those students, usually either watching movies or just talking. Often, once the lost students felt comfortable with us, our conversations turned to focus on God and faith.

Because of my roommate's position as an RA, he had a unique chance to witness to the other RAs in our dorm. One RA had grown up in church but never really had a relationship with Christ. He joined our Bible study at the beginning of the semester. One Sunday, I sat down with him for lunch in the dorm's café and shared the gospel with him. For some reason, he was really turned off and asked us never to talk to him about religion again. However, throughout the semester he gained a strong trust relationship with my roommate, his fellow RA. By the end of the year we saw that guy move from totally rejecting the gospel and pushing us away to accepting Christ as his Savior in April!

What really stuck out to me about our missional community is that the guys we spent time around and shared the gospel with would never have attended a campus ministry or church worship service. The reason we were able to engage them with the gospel was because we were going to them, investing in relationships with them where they already were rather than waiting for them to come to church with us.

In fact, most of the time these guys were resistant to actually attend any kind of Christian event but they felt comfortable enough around us to talk about our faith.

Raul Garcia recounts the formation of a missional community that was *not* primarily a group of Jesus followers but developed as part of building intentional spiritual conversations into a space that was part of a natural rhythm.

In spring 2004 I met Dave. He was training to be a college pastor at a local church and his first assignment was to lead a Bible study involving his peers, specifically the elite runners of our university's track team. As one of the premier athletes on the team, Dave had significant influence with his old teammates but he needed a friend to help him get things started. I obliged by helping him lay out a study plan for that semester as well as work through the options of where and how to start his missional community.

Instead of meeting in a church, we would meet in a place the team called home—the athlete's lounge. We chose to have our group on Tuesday, after the team's hard workouts, when we would offer free food and a chance to unwind after the most difficult stretch of the week. This process of moving toward the team's turf with an offer of spiritual exploration, instead of calling them away from familiar surroundings, really helped keep our group consistent and freshly stocked with friends who avoided churches on Sunday mornings.

Instead of a large group of Christians with nonbelievers coming in and out, we were populated with people who did not know Jesus, but wanted to learn more over pizza and conversation. Over the course of two years the small weekly meeting of athletes produced questions and answers that led to several conversions, multiple recommitments to God, and a general sense of spiritual openness on the team. Most encouraging of all was the eventual reproduction of our missional group. One student, who had been a part of our "track Bible study," eventually transferred to a new school. While there, she started a similar group for seekers on the women's cross-country team.

Rachel Alvarez took missional community "home" with her as her college missional community expression.

As a freshman, in 2006, I became a part of Campus Renewal Ministries. Through CRM I have been trained to be a missionary in my own community. Therefore, about a year ago I decided to move into student apartments with four of my friends who did not have a relationship with Jesus. With the partnership of other believers in the same complex I prayed for opportunities to share about Jesus to my roommates and neighbors. I was very open about my relationship in following Jesus. As a result one of my roommates became interested in learning more about him. We began to read the Bible one-on-one every day. A week into reading she accepted Jesus! We began a small group in our apartment where our roommates and neighbors would attend. There were six girls who consistently attended. That same semester, the entire small group decided to begin a relationship with Jesus. We have continued the small groups and one-on-one discipleship once a week.

The first girl who came to know Jesus, Natalie Plaza, has shared about her relationship with Jesus to her family. As a result her mother and brother have come to know Christ. Another girl, Neri Sanchez, is the president of the biggest Latin dance organization on campus. She has been inviting the members of the organization to receive prayer. Now her desire is to become a missionary abroad.

After five years of being a part of CRM, I feel well equipped to accomplish what God has destined for me to do, and that is to be a missionary to the nations.

That last phrase, "to be a missionary to the nations," captures the ultimate hope of the missional community experience—that students who learn to be missional community participants at UT Austin carry this passion and practice with them when they leave the college setting. Justin Christopher likes to quote Bill Bright, founder of Campus Crusade for Christ, who used to say: "Change the campus and you change the world." Justin goes on to say: "What if college students learn to live as missionaries on campus where they live, work, and play? If so, they will live on mission in our cities and around the world where they live, work, and play" (*Campus Renewal*, p. 162).

It looks like they are gaining traction in realizing that vision!

So why include a chapter detailing a campus missionary strategy involving missional communities? Because lots of congregations in America are bubbled off from their community. Because many people in those congregations still feel a burden to share the gospel but don't know how—and besides, they don't have relationships with people who are not church people. Maybe for them, the emphasis on becoming a missionary where they "live, work, and play" can find resonance. Maybe they can find others in their neighborhood, workplace, school, or social club who share a similar passion. Then just maybe they can form a missional community to support their missionary habit.

There is always the hope that some congregational leaders will see a missional community strategy as a possible way to move their ministry beyond helping people become good church members into helping people live lives on mission. Perhaps developing a Sparks Course might just be something they (you?!) want to do.

That could change the church. That then could change the world.

6

FUTURE TRAVELERS

MISSIONAL COMMUNITIES AS MEGACHURCH STRATEGY

"What if prevailing church models and leaders can become the major launching pad for new missional movements of the future ... ? What if there doesn't have to be a tyranny of the *or*—whether to be 'attractional' *or* 'incarnational'—but instead a genius of the *and*, where the strengths of the prevailing church platform are leveraged to release leaders capable of expanding the Kingdom *through new faith communities* [emphasis added]?"

These words framed the overview document for the first meeting of Future Travelers, convened in March 2010. The group had been recruited by Dave Ferguson and Todd Wilson of the Exponential Network. Sponsorship of the group was also provided by the Cornerstone Knowledge Network, established by Bill Couchenour and Ed Bahler. Alan Hirsch, founding director of Forge Mission Training Network and the author of numerous books giving shape to the missional movement, served as the facilitator. Other participants included Steve Andrews (Kensington Church, Troy, Michigan), Mark Beeson (Granger Community Church, Granger, Indiana), Brian Bloye (West Ridge Church, Atlanta, Georgia), Matt

Carter (the Austin Stone Community Church, Austin, Texas), Mark DeYmaz (Mosaic Church of Central Arkansas), Shawn Lovejoy (Mountain Lake Church, Cumming, Georgia), Greg Nettle (RiverTree Christian Church, Masillon, Ohio), Darrin Patrick (the Journey, St. Louis, Missouri), Todd Proctor (Rock Harbor, Orange County, California), Greg Surratt (Seacoast Church, Charleston, South Carolina), and Jeff Vanderstelt (Soma Communities, South Puget Sound, Washington).

Initially brought together so that pastors of multisite megachurches could enjoy some peer support, the group has become galvanized around a shared conviction that the megachurch must play a key role in the missional movement in North America. They have committed to a two-year process of experimentation and peer review, creating a learning community that will explore how to integrate incarnational missional movements into the current equation of church.

Alan Hirsch presented the group with what has become known as the 60–40 problem. Simply put, Hirsch contends that 60 percent of the American population is out of reach of the local church. These are unchurched and dechurched people who to varying degrees are alienated from the prevailing forms of church. Alan recalls, "This set the group on a journey to learn what it means to become a church that can reach the 60 percent as well as maintain its base among the 40 percent."

Future Travelers fully embraces a "both-and" approach to resolving the 60–40 problem. While continuing their attractional ministry approach, these church leaders are exploring ways of developing a church presence among people who will never "come to" church in a traditional sense. Hirsch and Dave Ferguson have written *On the Verge* (Zondervan, 2010) as a text to define the nature and scope of the program.

Each congregation is exploring the 60–40 problem in its own way and sharing its results with the group. Much experimentation and learning is under way. Some of the cohort downloaded their experience at the Exponential Conference in April 2011, which focused on the missional community development.

This chapter focuses on the missional community efforts of two of the Future Travelers cohort: the Austin Stone Church in Austin, Texas, and Community Christian Church, Naperville, Illinois, in Chicagoland. In both cases, the central learning is already clear: missional communities can thrive under the umbrella of the existing church. This exciting development further demonstrates the adaptability of this new post-congregational church life form.

Austin Stone—Morphing Missional

Click on the "What We Do" tab on the home page of Austin Stone Community Church (www.austinstone.org) and you will find "Missional Communities" as the first item in the drop-down box. A further click there brings you to a startling statement: "The Austin Stone is a network of missional communities—small groups of people, joined by the Gospel, pursuing the renewal and redemption of their community together. Missional community is the primary way to connect with others at the Austin Stone and pursue life on mission."

"Wait a minute!" you might say to yourself. "Isn't the Austin Stone a fast-growing megachurch begun by Matt Carter and Chris Tomlin in 2003 to reach college students through great worship and Bible teaching?" And you might further think, "Hasn't the church grown like crazy into more than seven thousand people gathering each weekend in eight worship services?" Which could lead you to wonder:

"So what's this stuff about being a 'network of missional communities'?"

If you went through that series of questionings you have identified a morphing process that is under way in this high-profile congregation in the Texas capital. According to Michael "Stew" Stewart, the pastor of Missional Community, the changes under way are the result of the church's determination not to grow consumers but to grow disciples of Jesus who are on mission with their lives. "We are not allergic to consumers—we love attracting thousands of curious people to Jesus. But we want to take a consumer to being missional," Stew commented. Then he added, "We asked ourselves, 'What does it look like for a missional church to be full of missional people'?"

Exploring the answer to that question has changed lots of things at the Stone.

Aha!s

With more than 2,500 people now in over 150 small groups, roughly 55 percent of the adult constituency of the Austin Stone is engaged in some way in a small group. Rather than disbanding all small-group expressions and starting over, the congregation is trying to move existing groups toward becoming missional communities. They are making progress. But it has been a steep learning curve.

Brought to the church as pastor of community groups in 2008, Stew recalls some huge "aha!" realizations that have paved the way for their journey into missional community development. First, church leaders realized that the efforts spent in developing the elements of an Acts 2 church in the community groups (worship, teaching, evangelism, and so on) had resulted in a discernible lack of community *or* mission!

Stew's study of church-planting movements around the globe that are successfully reproducing disciples brought the insight he needed to shift the approach from creating community groups to creating missional communities. In places like India and China, where growth is exponential, the church is focused on the mission of being ambassadors of Jesus, which is the storyline of the first chapter of Acts. The revelation was that all the missional community stuff in Acts 2 follows Acts 1, and Acts 1 is all about being on mission. "So the aha! moment for us," Stew recalls, "was the realization that when we aimed for community we got neither mission nor community. But when we started to aim for mission—community that is centered around the gospel—we got mission *and* community."

A second major aha! also came out of hitting a wall about eighteen months into the transition from community groups to missional communities. The church assumed that people knew how to live out the gospel. So, it was thought, all that was needed was some instruction. Stew tells it this way, looking back at that time. "Okay, missional communities, that's what we're going to do. Missional church. Missional people. Now go do it.... Go do these things. Go reach out here. Look for this. Go do this!" The result of all that exhortation and all that doing was that "we really kind of had a train wreck ... where leaders were burning out and people were burning out and flaming out and browning out."

The problem, Stew and others realized, was that they had ignored Paul's clear teaching that we live out the gospel based on our identity in Christ. Out of identity comes XYZ, the practices and behaviors associated with missional living; just doing XYZ won't produce the identity. The Stone was attempting to produce missional people without helping them process the questions of *How does the gospel change my identity?*

What does the gospel say to me? Then, *How does that work out for us in a group?* This insight has prompted a shift in training for leaders and missional community participants. They are no longer just shouting out the things to do; they are "gospel-centered in the way we motivate, in the way we train, in what our expectations are, in what we measure," Stew observes.

A third aha! has only recently been articulated. Again, it revolves around a probing question. This time it has to do with *How do we, in the Western church, develop community through small groups?* as opposed to *How do people who aren't engaged in a church develop community?* "We found that the *what*, the *how*, the *when*, and the *where* were completely different," Stew says.

For church small groups, community is built by sitting around in a circle talking about—yourself! Your hearts, your needs, your passion, your whatever—this is all "self" talk. It usually happens in someone's home or maybe a Sunday School class, with people sitting in a circle. It occurs once a week on a regular basis so that you wind up with setting aside two hours or so a week to go "be in community" with other church people.

How community is being developed by people who aren't in church is completely different. It's not done by sitting around in a circle doing "self" talk; rather, it happens side-by-side talking about other things, like politics, the weather, some project, or the game. It doesn't happen on some scheduled evening every week. It is based on the rhythms of their life, at their convenience. The *where* is different too because maybe a lot of times it is in a coffee shop or at an event, a concert, or a ball game.

Once this distinction was articulated an amazing truth emerged. Stew puts it this way: "When we are telling someone to come to our 'missional community,' you know, twelve people sitting around in a circle for two hours on Wednesday and you're calling that a mission community because you're inviting lost people ... who is actually being the missionary in the equation? Is it that group or is it the lost person?" Stew concludes that it is the lost people or the people not engaged in church who are being asked to be the missionary. They are being asked to give up the way they build community, where they build community, when they build community, to come do it with us. They are being asked to make all the sacrifices and change cultures so they can participate with us. If we claim to be a community of missionaries then we have to be willing to change our rhythms to match theirs. "You live and abide and incarnate in that context, do community how they would do it, and then just see what happens."

Coming to this realization has altered the way many of the missional communities are operating. One group in North Austin asked, "Hey, where does everybody go for coffee?" and began to focus their time and relationships there. They go as a group but they also go there when they're on a break or work downtown. As a result, they've gotten to know the manager and some of the regulars, which recently led a guy to become a follower of Jesus. This happened because they decided to join in where community is already present or forming. Instead of creating alternative block parties or an alternative National Night Out, missional communities join right into the neighborhood celebrations. The Austin missionaries are being trained to find out where their neighbors are eating so they go there to eat. That's what missionaries are expected to do overseas. That's what it takes to be missionaries here at home.

These aha! breakthroughs will likely not be the last in the process of becoming missional. After all, church as congregation has had centuries of practice to learn from.

Church as missional community is a new development, forcing new ways of thinking and behaving.

Logistics and Leaders

The Austin Stone missional communities gather on a weekly basis, although many gather more frequently, just to hang out, party, serve, meet people. The communities convene anywhere and anytime that matches the lifestyle rhythm of the group they are missionaries to.

Composed of four to twelve people, missional communities increasingly are the primary way the church's vision (Worship Christ, Live in Community, Get Trained for Ministry, Make Disciples) is lived out.

Key elements of their more structured gathered experience include eating together, worship, scripture reading, sharing life experiences, and typically some sort of life or spiritual discussion. Some groups discuss the weekend sermons from the larger gatherings. The church provides each leader with discussion questions based on the weekend messages. A growing number of the missional communities have smaller groups who meet separately for more in-depth exchange. Child care is handled in a variety of ways, from hiring child-sitters for all or part of the time to rotating community members, to taking care of children in another room of the house or nearby house, to total inclusion of children in the activities of the missional community when appropriate.

Leaders for missional communities both self-select (on the website people are invited to start a missional community) as well as being recruited from existing groups. This open-ended approach is an intentionally low bar setting for entry in order to allow lots of potential leaders to cross the threshold without being hazed out on the front end by too much commitment. However, the bar for remaining a leader is raised high through the leadership development process. The Austin Stone's mantra for developing leaders for these missional communities is "little by little, topic by topic, overtime and on the job." It is an ongoing and relentless process of increasingly intentional interfaces with the leader.

Todd Engstrom, who also works on staff as a pastor of missional community, remarks that leadership development begins with discipleship: "the first job is to make disciples of leaders." Todd's approach has been informed by his own experience of coming to Jesus through Young Life, with its emphasis on life transformation, along with his study of how church-planting movements train leaders worldwide. In countries where the gospel is exploding leaders are selected and trained while giving leadership. This differs sharply from a process of training people, then deploying them — more of a Western, academic approach. As a student at UT in Austin, Todd became acquainted with the missional community concept there and experienced the personal and group coaching process for missional community leaders.

Although the whole leadership coaching process is relationally oriented, there are well-planned processes for training leaders and lots of attention is paid to skill development. Peer learning groups of leaders meet on a monthly or bimonthly basis. These meetings focus on aspects of gospel, mission, and community. Three times a year there is a gathering of all the leaders, along with three meetings a year in each geographic region of missional communities.

Creating a Missionary Culture

Creating a missionary culture to support a missionary way of life is a key challenge and key strategy for leading the congregation through the missional transition. The leaders have implemented several key cultural components.

Global engagement, church leaders decided, could be reverse-engineered to help with the development of missionary DNA at home. For instance a key aspect for developing a missionary culture was for people to experience the "sent" aspect of being a missionary, a commissioning and commitment to a way of life. This is routinely experienced by those who go overseas on mission assignments. So the challenge became how to extend this sense of "sentness" to everyone in the congregation, even if they could not go overseas.

The Austin Stone is tackling this challenge through several strategies. First, they integrate international missions into everything they do; there is no separate missions department. They steer away from church-to-church partnerships or church-based programs, preferring instead to mobilize *people* into mission. Also, church leadership heavily emphasizes the need for missionaries to go to unreached people groups in the world. This call is routinely and systematically issued in worship services as well as in missional community settings, challenging and recruiting people literally to pick up and go live among these people groups. Some months ago the church set a goal of seeing one hundred people do this. This goal will be easily met. As of this writing, about thirty people have been already deployed, with another ninety committed to go, on top of more than fifty who are giving consideration to making this major life decision.

This goal, observes Joey Shaw, minister of international mission, "has created a structure." The structure is designed for nurturing missionary DNA throughout the congregation. Church leaders try to help everyone to see themselves as a "goer," a "sender," or a "mobilizer." Goers are obviously the ones who pack up, pick up, and go overseas. Not everyone can do this but everyone can be a sender and a mobilizer. Although you might not be able to go yourself, you can be part of a sender team who sends money and prayer and other resources as needed. Mobilizers help raise support among the members of their missional communities and also in the Austin area. Efforts are also made to establish links with refugee groups in the Austin area so that missional communities and people can engage with internationals and literally "go" without having to leave Austin.

Another part of the missionary culture strategy is the increasing development of short-term global mission opportunities for missional communities. These trips can be very effective in training participants on how to live as missionaries in their lives at home. Part of this emphasis comes out of Stew's personal background. Prior to coming to Austin he lived in under-resourced communities in Denton, Texas, and Memphis, Tennessee. His training for those settings came largely from Christian Community Development Association (CCDA), an organization started by John Perkins in the late 1960s to call mainly affluent and upwardly mobile African Americans to go back into at-risk black communities. CCDA has helped people understand how to live incarnationally. One of their core principles is "you can't commute to your ministry."

Stew has continued his practice of living in at-risk neighborhoods by moving into the St. John area of Austin, a very under-resourced part of the city. But he is not alone. Over fifty-five others from the Austin Stone have moved into the neighborhood as well, starting missional communities and figuring out how to incarnate the gospel. "The mission is the *what* and incarnation is the *how*," Stew says. "You can't separate those two. If you do missional without incarnation, you're not really doing mission; you're doing projects." And all of it is crosscultural if you are trying to plant the gospel in a context that is foreign to our culture.

There is no big strategic plan for the St. John area mission. The families are just doing what Jesus did as told by John in his first chapter. They are just taking their flesh and moving into the neighborhood. They live among, go to school with, make friends with, hang out with neighbors who need to know that Jesus loves them. And that his followers do, too. It's what the Stone calls the ministry of availability.

About two years ago a fire destroyed most of an apartment complex housing mainly immigrant families. Forty-five families were suddenly displaced. Stew and his family took in a single mom and two little girls. He tells what happened next: "Our missional community loved on her and served her and helped her. She ended up coming to Christ and we baptized her in our backyard in a baby pool, and you know, had fifty or sixty people here just cheering for her."

Austin Stone continues to shift from being a church *with* missional communities to being a church *of* missional communities. Right now, Stew admits, he is happy to see what develops as this new church life form finds expression. He also admits to not having a strategic plan. "Just being there and being present goes a long way to answering all the strategic questions we try to answer first. You're the missionary, so go to. Find their rhythms and go join them in what they're doing and live out. Just be available. Being present and being available go a long way to being missional."

Community Christian Church—Movementum

Yes, you read the word right—*movementum* is the term being used at this innovative megachurch started in Naperville, Illinois (now with eleven sites across Chicagoland), to describe what they are creating and experiencing in their journey toward becoming missional.

The story of Community Christian Church has been chronicled by founding brothers Dave and Jon Ferguson in their book *Exponential* (Zondervan, 2010). Practical innovation has been the name of the game from the get-go, driven by their passion of "helping people find their way back to God" (the church mission statement). The church focuses its interface with people through what they call the 3 Cs—celebrate, connect, and contribute—the three experiences they believe will help people's spiritual journey. The congregation helps people celebrate God through worship, connect with others through their small groups, and learn to contribute through service and stewardship. Each week's attendees are presented with one "Big Idea" of how they can live as followers of Jesus.

The result has been the creation of a highly attractive and contagious culture, a culture of "yes" rather than "no." This perspective not only characterizes the presentation of what it means to be a Jesus follower, but it also typifies an approach to ministry that promotes risks and innovation. People have responded in droves. About ten thousand people consider Community Christian their church home, with over six thousand people gathering for worship on any given weekend at one of the church's eleven locations. An ethos of "get-to" rather than "have-to" has created a spirit of adventure and joyful service. This explains in part why some successful business people give up their six-figure incomes for a fraction of their salaries so they can take jobs at the church. This attractiveness has also recruited hundreds of churches and thousands of church leaders into the Exponential Network (a multinetwork platform) and more recently the NewThing Network (a movement to foster churches that reproduce churches).

Community's vision forecasts their being a church of two hundred sites with one hundred thousand Jesus followers. Even if this vision is accomplished, church leaders realize that many of the nine million people in the Chicago area will never come to any church. These realities have propelled the leadership into exploring new approaches to help people celebrate, connect, and contribute without having to "come to church." Being proponents of "and" thinking instead of "either-or" thinking is allowing church leaders to consider new applications of church. The congregation's penchant for experimentation and learning creates an environment ripe for the emergence of missional communities.

"A shift in my thinking," reflects lead pastor Dave Ferguson, "came with ... the growing realization that even if we worked extremely hard and were fairly successful at planting lots of new churches and campuses there was still a certain percentage (I'm going to say at least 60 percent) that will never walk in the door of our churches no matter how cool and edgy they might be." This caused the church leadership to "rethink our strategy about mission and how we would accomplish that mission," Dave says.

That shift in strategy focused initially on the congregation's small group infrastructure. Small groups at Community have always been open, evangelistic, and reproducing. Most of the people becoming Jesus followers in the church's ministry (over four hundred baptized in 2010) come to faith in one of the more than three hundred adult small groups. Although many of the groups were engaging in missional activity, the leadership assessed that many of the people in the groups were not on mission in their personal lives. So every small group was challenged to become one of two types of groups:

- *Group with a mission:* These groups have a common cause as their affinity and they covenant to all be about the accomplishment to that mission.

- *Group with missionaries:* These groups have a relational affinity and they covenant to hold each other accountable for the individual missions that God has called them to.

The expectation is that every person in each group will individually covenant to be on mission and that every group will covenant together for their missional expression.

This missional covenanting is the key strategy for turning existing small groups into missional communities. Dave comments, "We now believe God is calling us to mobilize every one of those people for mission. It is our goal and belief that in the coming year that the number of people on mission will be 100 percent of our weekend celebration service attendance."

67–20 Strategy

Efforts for creating missional communities don't just focus on recovenanting existing small groups. The movementum for creating missional communities also involves new expressions of church.

Kim Hammond has been brought in from Australia's Forge Network (a ministry of training church planters for incarnational ministry) to serve as Community's director of missional imagination. Working alongside Carter Moss and Eric Metcalf, Community's small groups champion, they are plowing new territory in starting missional communities. These groups operate with a different scorecard than typical church ministries that measure church-based activity. These missional communities are community-centric, not church-centric, and therefore help people figure out how to celebrate, connect, and contribute beyond church walls. As Kim says, "innovation in the past has been focused on church structures (like the multisite strategy); the next chapter is about focusing innovation on the outside."

The newest such innovation is the development of the 67–20 strategy and rhythm for small group ministry. This emphasis goes beyond merely rebranding existing small-group approaches. It is an intentional reorientation of small groups that requires different content and different rhythms than in the past.

The numbers help tell the story of what is involved. The number "67" is the percentage of the population in the Chicagoland area that is "far from God." This number is derived from a combination of church attendance and polling of religious beliefs and attitudes of people in the area (in *Exponential* the Ferguson brothers say less than 20 percent of the nation's population is in church any given Sunday). This 67 percent of the population forms the target group for the new missional community strategy. The people in this group represent a different constituency than the people who come to worship each week and want a small-group experience for discipleship, which is more the typical church culture person. Connecting with these "unconnected" people is going to require a different rhythm of group life than one that works for the already churched.

The number "20" in the 67–20 strategy stands for the percentage of the world that lives in poverty, on less than $2 per day. Incorporating this number into the new group strategy raises awareness of peoples' plights and our call to be restorative agents by loving our neighbors, loving the poor, and addressing societal ills. This emphasis calls each group to some engagement with issues of social justice or ministry to the "least of these." The interface might be overseas; it could just as easily be local. The target group doesn't have to be destitute but it is to be a part of the community that is economically challenged.

In January 2011 the church launched the Jesus Mission 67–20 initiative to raise awareness with all its constituents of this new focus and direction. Among the ways the church introduced this emphasis was the invitation for members to try to eat on $2 per day for one week. Suggestions and even recipes were posted on the website to help those who took this challenge. The idea was to help members experience some of the challenges faced by those less fortunate. This approach is typical to Community—presenting a "Big Idea" designed to help people do something different to experience the truth offered in their teaching.

Putting This All Together—in Aurora

Just a couple of miles from Community's Naperville home campus (fondly called *the Yellow Box* for its color and architectural design) lies the community of Aurora. It is a very different city than its upscale neighbor, with great ethnic diversity and considerable patches of economically challenged older neighborhoods mixed in with brand-new planned communities. Two stories will flesh out how the new missional community strategy is playing out—in very different ways—in this city not far away from the church's first location, but light years away from being "churched" at the Yellow Box.

The first is Kim Hammond's Hometown initiative involving multiple 67–20 groups in a new housing development in Aurora (called *Hometown*). "We didn't start with a 'church' in mind; so we're starting with a different scorecard and strategy," he comments. Kim approached the building developer of a new housing project, offering to be the community developer for the neighborhood. The building developer agreed. Kim began with ten weeks of T-ball in order to build relationships with the people of the development. It was hugely successful and three groups were initially birthed out of those interfaces. Apprentice leaders are already being developed with the expectation that these initial groups will reproduce. Currently these missional communities meet in homes.

The missional communities have adopted a monthly rhythm and an annual strategy. On week one, the group meets together for study and to celebrate how God is showing up in the lives of the people of the community. Week two is given to purposeful connection with neighbors through backyard barbecues or house parties. The third week gathering celebrates new connections (because new people have come into the community typically). Weeks two and three really focus on the 67 percent population. Week four is given to some kind of external ministry—keeping the "20" background in mind—so the missional community serves together in some way to contribute to the neighborhood. Many people face economic challenges in the Aurora area so there are plenty of local opportunities.

The missional communities also plan to use four big holidays a year—Easter, July 4, Halloween, and Christmas—to create big neighborhood events. This approach is especially attractive to the large Hispanic population, which tends to love large family gatherings.

The goal is not to move these missional communities into the Yellow Box. They are incarnational communities that connect with each other to form a network church specific to Hometown. This is not the only one of these incarnational initiatives under way. Another effort targets downtown Chicago, a much different inner-city environment that will require the development of an indigenous strategy contextualized to that area. However, the same 67–20 strategy will serve as a guide for group life.

A second church initiative in the East Aurora area has been under way for several years. However, it didn't start as a small group. It began with the passion of one family, who decided to reverse course and intentionally execute a down-wardly mobile life change.

A self-described "social activist" in college, Kirsten Strand, now a wife and mother of two, became a Christian in grad school. She immediately saw a disconnect between evangelical church practice and its lack of engagement with the community's social needs. As a member of Community, exploring what the church could do outside its walls, she attended a Christian Community Development Association (CCDA) conference in 2001 that "wrecked" her life (in a good way, she adds). She became convinced that community development, not just drive-by acts of compassion, was the answer to making long-term systemic change in East Aurora.

Kirsten approached the elementary school in the area and asked, "how can we help?" She became aware that 80 to 90 percent of kids at the school were on the free lunch program, a reality that signaled she had entered a different world from affluent Naperville where she lived. Her initial school engagement was to help provide a Christmas Gift Mart. People from the church were asked to donate toys that could be sold for a small fraction of their cost. By charging a small amount the project allowed the parents to preserve their dignity by purchasing Christmas presents for their families. The proceeds of the sale were then invested back into the community, distributed to some existing community agencies that serve the poor in the area. This was an instant success, a "win-win" Kirsten says, and continues now several years later (in 2010 over 9,500 toys were collected, 1,100 volunteers were involved, and $11,300 was raised for distribution to the community partners).

Kirsten and Scott (her husband) became convinced that serving East Aurora was requiring them to do more than drive in and out of the area on various ministry projects. They decided they needed to live in the community, a move that would require several years of preparation. Scott quit his job as a regional sales rep and went back to school to earn a teaching degree so he could teach in the Aurora school system. Kirsten took on a part-time job at Community, allowing her to pursue her passion and to galvanize others into this ministry, but also to help pay the bills while Scott was in school. She was able to start Community 4:12 (based on Ecclesiastes 4:12), a ministry with a mission of "uniting people to restore communities."

The Strands moved into East Aurora in 2008, enrolling their school-aged kids into a school where theirs were the only white students at the time. The move turned out to be "the biggest blessing we'd ever experienced," according to Kirsten. Their credibility skyrocketed in the community, with people knowing that they were not working "for them," but "for us" in their community development efforts. In addition, Kirsten's authenticity has challenged many more people at Community to become involved in Community 4:12. Now full-time on church staff, Kirsten leads this ministry to partner with six elementary schools, a middle school, and a high school with after-school programs, tutoring, and parent training. She also works with other nonprofits in the area to help them achieve their mission of building the community. A facility to house Community 4:12 has been secured. A bilingual campus plant of Community was started in 2010.

The Strands are no longer alone in their relocation. Another young couple has moved from Naperville into East Aurora, with two to three other couples contemplating it. Half a dozen missional communities have been birthed, some a mix of Hispanic-Anglo families. People even from other neighborhoods have made the new church their choice of spiritual community. Some are beginning to be in small groups with people from the East Aurora area. As more and more people are exposed to the challenges of the under-resourced community, more and more people are being infected with the missional virus. "For the Yellow Box," Kristen says, "missional community is a small group on mission. Out here, all of life is missional."

What does the Strands' story have to do with missional communities? Through their incarnational presence and ministry they have paved the way into a part of the city that is now wide open to the missional community approach. It shows the power of a person or family to create breakthroughs that change entire communities—and church cultures. Through their passion and obedience the Strands have created movementum—helping people see it, get it, and do it.

The missional community strategy is changing the scorecard for Community Christian. "The small group strategy in the past has largely served the gathering—a part of an attractional-only approach," Eric reflects. "Now we are going to figure out how to celebrate 3 C Christ followers who don't connect with our existing church." He is encouraged at the response so far. "It's unreal how this move resonates with people and within people."

Future Travelers have embarked on a journey of exploration and discovery. They intend to show how the North American megachurch can champion the emergence of missional communities. They bring megaresources to bear and expect megaresults! Their approach celebrates the synergy between church as congregation and church as missional community.

7

MISSION HOUSTON

MISSIONAL COMMUNITIES FOR SPIRITUAL FORMATION AND COMMUNITY TRANSFORMATION

In September 2007 a group of eighteen people came together for a three-day retreat near Houston, Texas. Their gathering was birthed out of two shared convictions: first, that the church needed to be making more of a positive impact in the community beyond its walls; and second, that personal transformation results in and accelerates community transformation. This story of Mission Houston tells what has come out of that retreat.

Our previous examples of missional communities have all focused on what is involved in creating them—from the architecture of the groups to the recruitment and training of leaders to the development of community rhythms and activities. The hope behind these efforts is that by fashioning the right approach to missional communities, missional followers of Jesus will be formed. The path has led from the missional communities to the individual disciple.

What if the approach to developing missional communities were turned around? In other words, what if the path began with individuals, then processed to the formation of missional communities? What if the primary focus and energy went into the development of missional followers of Jesus, with the expectation that missional communities would follow?

This second strategy is exactly how the Mission Houston team has gone about developing missional communities. "Our approach to creating missional communities has been to create and engage people in a deep spiritual formation process," says Jim Herrington, founding director.

The process, called *Faithwalking,* is the product of Jim's own spiritual journey. Raised up in church in rural Louisiana, Jim became a youth pastor at age nineteen, going on to serve four churches in two city contexts. In 1989 he became the executive director of the largest local association of Southern Baptist churches in the United States, the Union Association of greater Houston, comprising more than five hundred congregations at the time. "During that period," Jim reflects, he observed that the church was having "less and less positive impact in our city."

This growing reality launched Jim and a group of friends on a journey. "Shaped by the questions, *What is a disciple of Jesus?* and *How do you make one?* we worked to get clarity on the distinction between a church member and a follower of Jesus," he recalls. Faithwalking is the "sum and the substance" of the answers they came up with to those two questions.

"Houston—We've Got a Problem ... and an Opportunity!"

The Mission Houston story didn't start with Faithwalking. There were previous chapters. Jim Herrington and others founded Mission Houston in 1998, with the goal of helping congregations move beyond "Constantinian triumphalism" (as Jim puts it) into being salt and light so that the community at large can experience the kingdom of God. From

1998 through 2005 Jim labored for this by working through congregations, focusing on church leaders. During 2006 Jim experienced a time of significant depression that drove him to rethink his strategy. In early 2007 a group of business-men, self-styled *revolutionaries* (a term taken from George Barna's book *Revolution*), convinced Jim to focus his work on lay people and the creation of missional communities. They were the initial group who came together for a retreat in September of that year to begin a three-year pilot project aimed at community transformation—beginning with per-sonal transformation. The pilot project, called *Faithwalking*, has revolutionized Mission Houston.

Faithwalking is now a journey of spiritual and personal formation, reflecting the biblical perspective that we were created to be faith walkers (2 Corinthians 5:7). The journey always begins with a three-day inaugural retreat (Faithwalking 101). At the conclusion of that retreat experience par-ticipants are invited to become part of a twenty-six-week small-group experience (Faithwalking 201). The participants involved in Faithwalking typically have been recruited or recommended by someone who has experienced the process. Their expectations of what they will experience have been shaped by people whose lives have been profoundly affected through the courses.

The focus of both Faithwalking components centers on helping people understand and develop a missional life. The retreat lays out a pathway to personal transfor-mation and the twenty-six-week experience prepares the participant to become part of a missional community. Both components—Faithwalking 101 and 201—provide a guided spiritual transformation process (which will be detailed in this chapter). Curriculum for the retreat and the subsequent process have been fleshed out by Jim Herrington, along with

Steve Capper, managing director for Mission Houston, and Trisha Taylor, also a director with the organization.

Expectations are that those who complete Faithwalking 101 and 201 will then either join or start a missional community. The missional community is a continuation of the participants' spiritual formation, turning its focus to community transformation by the group's contribution to the common good of the city. Each missional community (tending to be composed of five to nine people) discerns its common service direction and venue—its mission—acting as catalysts to improve people's lives as a kingdom expression. Their goal is not multiplication of the missional community itself. Nor is it evangelism, at least not in the typical evangelical approach, though they do recruit others to join them in their mission, not all of whom are Jesus followers. Their purpose is to serve a need or people group for the long haul, not just work on "projects"—to be salt and light in the community so that it experiences the kingdom of God coming on earth as it is in heaven.

Missional communities function in a variety of ways. Regardless of how often they gather, they are encouraged to focus on two things. One focus of their energy is on advancing their mission by addressing key questions. What are the needs? How are we doing? Are we reaching our goals? What things are we measuring? What adjustments need to be made? The other focus of the community centers on strengthening relationships among members of the missional community. Whose story have we not heard? Can we do that over a shared meal? Is there any conflict we need to attend to? How are we each holding up under this load? How can we pray for one another?

Many, if not most, missional community participants retain their congregational affiliation if they have one (not all do). The goal of Mission Houston is not to replace congregations with missional communities but to supplement and strengthen their capacity. Just last year (2010) five different congregations, independent of each other, approached Mission Houston with the request that it help them "deploy our people for missional living." In one congregation that had a cohort going through Faithwalking at the time of this writing, ten participants indicated their intentions to launch ten *different* missional communities at the end of their journey together!

The core tenet of Faithwalking is that as we live missionally we become fully human and fully alive. Life is meant to be expressed on and through mission. Understanding Mission Houston's approach to missional communities revolves around grasping this key conviction.

Faithwalking 101

The foreword of the notebook used at the Faithwalking 101 three-day retreat expresses a yearning, followed by a conviction. First, the yearning: "[I]t is our clear intention to develop a community of transformational leaders who can be used by God as He reverses decades of declining impact of The Church" (p. 2). How will this be accomplished? That's where the conviction comes in. "Faithwalking focuses on the process of personal transformation that results in and accelerates community transformation." The end goal of the experience is "the multiplication of transformed and transforming leaders who are leading missional communities in families, neighborhoods, communities, work places, and third places of our city" (Faithwalking Notebook [FWN] 101:24).

The Mission Houston team decided to spell out the results they are seeking through their spiritual formation process. What they came up with serves as their purpose statement:

> Faithwalking is creating a community of disciples of Jesus who are being personally transformed and becoming catalysts mobilizing Christians to become the functioning Body of Christ in their homes, neighborhoods, workplaces, and third places to serve the poor, the marginalized, and those in need to work for the common good and to restore individuals, social systems, communities, and nations to God's design.

Bringing this about, the Mission Houston teams asserts, will require working "from a new mental model that guides our understanding of discipleship and service to the common good."

St. Irenaeus's famous declaration, "The glory of God is a human fully alive," expresses a truth demonstrated most clearly in Jesus's incarnation. However, it was a truth meant to be lived by all of us. Jesus made it clear to his followers that he had come to give them this abundant life (John 10:10). The missional life is the abundant life.

The problem is that the contemporary view of what it means to be fully human, fully alive is in direct odds to the biblical view of how this is achieved. Western culture commends a self-centered, consumerist approach to the abundant life. As it says in the Faithwalking notebook: "In this view a growing life of ease and convenience is the goal; suffering and sacrifice are to be avoided when possible. It's a self-centered life where I take care of me and mine but ignore the poor, the marginalized, the oppressed" (FWN 101:6). We define ourselves "by what is possessed and consumed" (FWN 101:6).

Jesus's approach to the abundant life was to remind us of our call to a life of service and stewardship. We are responsible for ourselves, our families, and also for our neighbors to serve them. We are also created to exercise stewardship over the earth, meaning that we are responsible for the common good—the systems and structures of the community we live in. This means the common good is our assignment and "when we take on that assignment we experience the fully human, fully alive reality that Jesus says is possible" (FWN 101:6).

2 Chronicles 7:14 makes a clear connection between the condition of "the land" (the common good) and the quality of our discipleship. When God's people live fully into their design not only do we experience the abundant life Jesus promises, but also the common good flourishes. The many societal ills that afflict our culture, from the breakdown of the family to the existence of institutionalized poverty to the challenges of our educational system, point to a problem with God's people—our failure to be fully human, fully alive.

This perspective provides the "new mental model" that serves as the underpinning for the Mission Houston strategy and process for creating missional communities. The "Mental Model to Transformation" has three components:

- Radical obedience—which leads to a missional life
- A reflective life—where you increasingly co-create the world with God
- Authentic community—which leads to shared vision

These components are not linear or compartmentalized—they interact and shape each other. These three central ideas are unpacked in the Faithwalking process. The content and dynamics of both the Faithwalking 101 retreat and the Faithwalking 201 small-group experience weave in and out of these three components.

Radical Obedience—A Missional Life

Sadly, the cultural consumerist view has infiltrated the church, greatly diminishing our capacity to act as salt and light. Many congregations see themselves as purveyors of religious goods and services, and church members behave as consumers of religious programming. The call to radical obedience to Jesus, to live a life of service and stewardship, has been largely absent from our conversations.

The Faithwalking journey confronts this reality head-on. In the process of the weekend retreat, participants are offered key insights into how we come to develop a life of disobedience. Sometimes we consciously and willfully act rebellious in our decisions. But oftentimes we are acting out on "vows" we made as children—how we had to be in the world to be safe (shy, gregarious, cautious, adventurous, and so on)—decisions we made usually in response to some hurt or embarrassment or neglect. We have practiced these vows so long that they have become habitual behaviors. Some of these vows are in direct violation of the teachings of Jesus. We have to figure out what these are in our lives so that we can change our behavior (repent) and go free from their enslavement.

Addressing disobedience is not a matter of feeling guilt and shame or condemnation and judgment. God's perspective is more akin to that of a wise and loving parent who knows what is better for us and wants us to experience it. As we take on lives of radical obedience, God reveals to us what we don't now "see" in terms of how these vows are getting in the way of our being able to experience life fully.

We must make two changes in order to live missionally. We can no longer tolerate the compartmentalization of our life or the individualization of our faith. A life of radical obedience will require a repudiation of both old ways of living. A missional life is one in which our lives are integrated into one coherent whole rather than segmented into disconnected, separated parts. We bring all our energies, passions, and resources to the pursuit of the kingdom of God. Life on mission will take place where we spend most of our waking hours—our homes, our workplaces. Understanding this will allow us to uncompartmentalize our approaches to spiritual development, positioning us to listen for and look for God in our everyday lives and everyday places. But we must also realize that we are not on this mission alone. This journey is not intended to be a private one. Connecting with the body of Christ is the only way we can function in the way God intended us to live.

A great example of this kind of life integration through mission is the development of missional communities at the Kirby Corporation (KC), a company based in Houston focused on marine transportation. An initial Bible study group of four people has grown into a "living Body of Christ at KC," according to Jerry Gallion, who chronicles the story on the Mission Houston website (www.missionhouston.org). A companywide intercessory prayer team hosts a weekly conference call open to anyone in the company and anyone on one of the hundreds of ocean vessels around the world. Disaster relief teams deployed after hurricanes Katrina and Rita helped throughout the Gulf Coast to address the needs of seven hundred Kirby families affected by these storms. Community service projects are now part of the company culture as well as groups paying attention to the daily needs of coworkers. Followers of Jesus are living out their faith in their primary engagement, their workplace.

A Reflective Life—Co-create the World with God

We are not able to live lives of radical obedience without abiding in Jesus. Abiding allows Jesus's life to flow from the vine to the branch (John 15:5). Jesus's life in us creates a right view of ourselves, our relationships, and the world around us. These insights come through developing a life of reflection. Reflective living maintains a relationship with Jesus that is dynamic and continuous. It is a way of life required for missional living.

The daily practice of the spiritual disciplines offers a way to develop a reflective lifestyle. These disciplines, used by the church throughout history, are solitude, worship, prayer, fasting, study, confession, giving, and celebration. Dabbling in these disciplines will not work. Adding these disciplines to an already overcrowded and over-busy life might produce some short-term change and heightened connection with Jesus. However, for genuine transformation to occur, these disciplines must become a way of life. Other things in our lives probably will have to be sacrificed in order to make room for these practices.

Spiritual disciplines are not a "to-do" list to achieve spiritual maturity. Checklists of spiritual activity cannot in and of themselves be measures of maturity. After all, the Pharisees had checklists but no transformation. Spiritual disciplines are designed to be relational activities. This is the secret of their transformative power. They do their "work" when we engage them while being honest with ourselves and transparent in disclosing ourselves to God. By allowing God access to our "secret" selves, we place ourselves in a position of being transformed. By practicing authenticity with God we move more and more into an intimate, not just personal, relationship with him. We bring "all of ourselves we know to all we know of God" (FWN 101:49). We experience his power to deal with our darkest and neediest selves. We are transformed.

Faithwalking 201 really helps participants routinely practice the spiritual disciplines by its homework assignments, beginning with a declaration by each person of the "spiritual workout" they intend to conduct for the duration of the experience. This encompasses a daily, weekly, and occasional schedule of which ones of the spiritual disciplines the member will practice and how they will be pursued. For instance, some days might be slotted to include a period of solitude or this practice might be reserved for a longer experience on some monthly rhythm. The same would be true for the other disciplines.

Authentic Community—Shared Vision

The scriptures reflect an expectation that we will not only be intimately connected with Christ, but also with each other. This level of relationship typically doesn't happen in our contemporary church culture, where "church" has become a few hours of spiritual spectatorship a week mostly involving watching other people do some things. This compartmentalization and privatized notion of discipleship has robbed us of the prayer support, collective wisdom, and accountability that is required for genuine life transformation.

Simply adding group activities to life does not bring about transformation. It requires a conscious choice to reorient life around community, even sacrificing other things in order to achieve it. Developing and maintaining authentic community must be a way of life.

Although the idea of authentic community is appealing, it can also be threatening. Maybe we don't trust others. It might take massive doses of a loving and trustworthy community to undo the skepticism and distrust we have developed from experiences in our families of origin or through the years with others who judged, criticized, and shamed us—including other Christians. In addition, submitting our lives to others challenges our need for control.

As the master discipler, Jesus did not make disciples by writing a book or teaching formal classes. He created a community in which people could enjoy a relationship with him while pursuing a kingdom mission. This is still needed by missional followers of Jesus. "We need a community of support that regularly and persistently holds up Jesus's countercultural view of what it means to be fully human" (FWN 101:78). Although the personal choice to be a missional Jesus follower is essential, it needs the consistent reinforcement of a community of support to be sustained and faithfully lived out.

Mission Houston's missional community strategy is designed to integrate and reinforce all three elements of transformation. Participants are helped to embrace lives of radical obedience by practicing disciplines that result in a reflective life, lived out through a supporting and authentic community.

Providing Accountability

The Mission Houston team maintains a core conviction that accountability is essential to the journey of transformation. This is why, at the conclusion of the Faithwalking 101 retreat, they offer three levels of accountability for people as they journey on into a life of mission. People are not asked or encouraged to leave the congregations where they are members. However, the Mission Houston approach acknowledges that not everyone is in a congregation that makes personal spiritual transformation and community transformation a priority.

Level One

Faithwalking 201—the twenty-six-week small-group experience—allows people who have completed Faithwalking 101 to continue the journey toward personal transformation.

The groups meet every other week (twelve sessions) for one hour and fifteen minutes. Homework outside of class takes about one hour per week (the "daily workout" involving some aspect of practicing the spiritual disciplines plus work on the broken aspects of personal relationships). All of the themes introduced in Faithwalking 101 are reinforced. In addition, the small group deals with key personal issues related to the formation of a missional community in the group's lives—learning to see and manage anxiety that can affect community, as well as identifying defensive reactions that prevent community, dealing with negative emotions, and learning to dialogue in community.

Level Two

When participants begin the small-group experience, they each are assigned a personal transformation coach. The coach has a weekly conversation with them and one other Faith-walker on a conference call. The coach's purpose is to provide encouragement, accountability, and additional resources if people get stuck in the process.

Level Three

At the conclusion of Faithwalking 201, participants are challenged to either join an existing missional community or to launch a new one in the place where they spend most of their working day. This approach helps them overcome the compartmentalization and privatization of spirituality that has contributed to the church's ineffectiveness in our culture. Placing missional community in the center of life also provides a high degree of accountability and support for living a missional life. Becoming part of a missional community calls into play all that has been learned in the Faithwalking 101 and 201 experiences.

Each missional community has a coach who teaches for community transformation, including how each missional community has decided to develop metrics for measuring its activities and impact. The leaders of the missional communities are introduced to Jim Collins's *Good to Great and the Social Sector* (2005, HarperCollins), and taking the suggestions he makes, they identify three key measures:

- *Inputs.* These are actions that missional communities engage in to get an output. Examples of inputs include mobilizing a team of volunteers to mentor schoolchildren, connecting with the school principal, sending out flyers to parents.
- *Outputs.* These are results that should lead to long-term transformational outcomes. For example, the previously mentioned inputs should yield specific mentoring outputs, which would include the number of kids who get mentored and the impact on their school attendance and on their grades.
- *Outcomes.* These are the long-term, transformational changes that affect individuals (students and family members becoming Jesus followers, succeeding in education, forming healthy families) and communities (high functioning of various community and social systems, such as education and law enforcement).

Each missional community devises and tracks its own measures.

For Leaders

Leaders of the missional communities have additional resources and accountability provided by Mission Houston.

When first starting a missional community they participate in a weekend retreat that focuses on the practical issues they will face in leading the group. Leaders have a personal coach to walk with them through the process of launch as well as access to the coach who is assigned to their missional community. Four times a year the leaders of all the communities gather for a celebration and training time. They eat together, welcome new retreat graduates, share stories of success, problem-solve common issues, and worship.

The End Game—What's Going On

How is the Mission Houston pilot project progressing? So far 68 percent of those completing Faithwalking 101 and 201 have either begun or become involved with a missional community. That 2007 retreat has been followed by fifteen additional retreat cohorts of 191 participants, who have given birth to over thirty missional communities. The retention rate of communities is excellent. To date, no missional community that has been a part of the pilot project has ceased to exist.

Here are five examples of the more than thirty missional communities currently engaged with Mission Houston in terms of their missional focus and how they are gauging their effectiveness.

Fifth Street

This missional community, led by Todd and Denise McCombs, is on mission in one of the most economically impoverished neighborhoods in Houston. There are currently ten adult members. These members joined alongside an existing community ministry that offered a food distribution program and an after-school Bible club ministry for students in the neighborhood. The missional community has helped to increase the amount of food delivered and to widen the distribution. Some of the missional community members serve as mentors to students in the local school once a week for an hour during the school day. Others serve as after-school tutors to students, joined by a few others outside the missional community membership. Fifth Street community has also started a low- or no-cost sports program, beginning with basketball. The program offers training to the children, as well as participation in competitive games. A Hispanic member of the missional community who is a paralegal and ex-offender addresses immigration questions and needs, including counseling and helping fill out and file paperwork for work permits and residency. The missional community is tracking the number of children mentored, the number of children in sports clubs, and the number of people served through their immigration information service.

Kingdom Advisors

Led by Randy Schroder, a financial advisor, and members of his staff, this missional community has several objectives. The first is to equip Christians in the financial advising profession to transform their industry by modeling personal integrity in exemplifying and teaching biblical generosity. Second, Kingdom Advisors also teaches biblical stewardship to children and youth, with the long-term goal of developing generous people who bless the community. Finally, the group works to help investors maximize financial impact through the support and underwriting of effective and sustainable efforts that address needs with the City of Houston.

The Church in the Mobile Home Park

A wealthy retiree, looking to retreat on his acreage outside of town, was challenged by God to buy and fix up a nearby run-down mobile home park. Bob and Cathie Baldwin now lead a group of four adults and three teenagers on mission in a forty-unit mobile home park, serving the residents there. They have constructed new roads, built a community development center, started a Hispanic church, and are working on developing nearby green space for recreation. The missional community is determined to stop the cycle of poverty of this population in this generation and to build common grounds of relationship and experience between the mobile home people and their affluent neighbors. A family of bilingual members of the missional community live in a home on the mobile home property, serving as educational, emotional, and spiritual counselors to park residents. The long-term metrics of the community involve assessing the impact on the lives of children (through grades, graduation, and jobs). They have started a summer work program for kids and outfitted the community center with computers for classes with kids and adults.

Love Works

Josh and Aimee Wood lead this missional community of seven mostly young adults who live together in a community setting and serve Gregory Lincoln Education Center, a public elementary school where 91 percent of the kids are below the poverty level. They are tracking the number of children being mentored and the long-term educational and social improvement of those mentored.

Yellowstone Academy

Yellowstone Academy is a school for children of low-income parents and families whose goal is to deliver the children (and their families) from generational poverty through quality education, tutoring, and mentoring. The community, led by Steve and Karen Capper, gathers once a month from 6:30–7:30 AM to walk the grounds and halls of the school, praying as they do for the students, teachers, and families. Requests by staff as well as the ongoing observations of the group from their engagement inform these prayers. *Shepherds* (their term for mentors) in the group have adopted ten students for every-other-week meetings in homes and for outings. Others have adopted two single parents as advocates and mentors. The community is helping with the school's online and in-print communications, is sponsoring a Brownie Scout troop for all second-grade girls, and periodically provides chaperones for school functions. Metrics being tracked by the missional community include inputs (number of volunteers assisting the staff during the school day or helping with after-school activities, as well as the number of on-site and off-site intercessors) and outputs (student academic and social performance, graduation rates and postsecondary education, and the longevity of highly evaluated faculty and staff).

The approach of Mission Houston seems validated by the experiences of those involved. Steve Capper, the managing director, serves as an example. Steve came to Houston in 1994 with the dream of working with other Christians to address the needs of the city. He first worked as a rector of an inner-city declining congregation but experienced great frustration in his inability to build a coalition of people willing to tackle community issues. He then became part of the Mission Houston team, drawn to its focus on spiritual formation. Discouragement has given way to hope. He capsules his latest learnings with these two observations:

> One, the brokenness that characterizes our communities and cities (and nation and Church) did not happen overnight,

and they are not going to be healed overnight. The work of establishing shalom in demonstrably beneficial and pervasive ways will require desperate, informed and united prayer and it will require [credits to Eugene Peterson] a long obedience in the same direction.

Second, and related, the majority of the members of the Body of Christ are not currently capable of sustaining either intercession or selfless serving. Unless we are being transformed, we will be the biggest roadblocks to the wealth of great ideas and good will among us.

These observations reveal two enormous challenges. Mission Houston takes square aim at both through their approach to developing missional communities.

8

LOOKING AHEAD

Rather than write a conclusion to wrap up the discussion of missional communities I want to open up some new conversation! I want to do some forecasting about where this development may be headed and how it might proceed along the way.

First, let me say some things I did not say—as well as reiterate some things I did declare. I *did not* say that church as congregation was going away. The term *post-congregational church* is meant to imply a new chapter of church expression, not that all existing and former church expressions are going away. What I *did say is that church* as congregation may have reached its market saturation. None of this is meant to diminish what church as congregation means to the millions of people who attend each week and find their spiritual needs met by traditional church.

I also *did not* say that congregational church is a bad form of church. I *did* point out some of its limitations for connecting with today's culture, particularly for those not already congregationalized. *I did* suggest that many people will no longer choose or be able to choose to pursue their spiritual journey by matching their lives with a congregational church rhythm. For these people missional communities might be the way they experience church. And I *did* argue that we need to expand the bandwidth of how we think church can be expressed in this culture, especially because the number of people susceptible to being congregationalized is dwindling. Finally, I plead guilty of asserting that the advent of missional communities affords us a hopeful future of releasing church from its institutional moorings, allowing it to recapture its initial expression as a street movement.

Missional communities represent a way for the church to be incarnationally present in people's lives right where they already are, in the rhythms of the life they are already living. People no longer allow record companies or TV network programmers to dictate how or when they can enjoy their music or watch their favorite television show. The same is increasingly true in people's spiritual journeys. Missional communities allow participants to customize their spiritual development. Some people will prefer more scripting than others. Some will prefer more study and discussion and others will choose to express their faith more actively through service. These preferences will not likely remain static as people go through different chapters of their lives.

Having said (and not said) some things, here are a few hunches and discussion starters for further investigation.

Missional Communities Won't Develop as Plug-and-Play Applications

The stories I chose for inclusion in this book represent a wide range of expression of missional communities—as a church-planting strategy, an architectural fractal for a network church, an evangelism strategy to reach a particular people group, an outreach strategy for existing (and highly successful) congregations, and as a vehicle for spiritual formation and community transformation. Not once was the word *model* used in telling the tales. The point is not to suggest a template of your (or anyone's) approach to developing missional communities. The hope is to excite your imagination so you can consider your own possibilities for exploring this new expression of church. Church as missional community is incarnational and contextual. There is no garden variety missional community; however, there *is* a garden of variety in store as new iterations emerge.

Let me suggest some trends and factors that are on the horizon.

- Many of the missional communities in these stories still revolve around the congregation. This will continue to be true, especially as missional communities are adopted as a megachurch strategy for reaching people who are not being reached by traditional congregational approaches. Megachurches set trends that others follow, so I fully expect them to give lots of congregational leaders the permission to begin thinking about including missional communities as part of their ministry portfolio.

- Missional communities will speed up the development of the network church. The network church is manifesting in multiple ways. Multisite strategies (again, largely a megachurch innovation) created a new operating platform to move the church past a mainframe operation. Other iterations on the macro level will include the formation of city churches coming together primarily for serving the community and for expressions of church designed to celebrate and pursue common mission. The city churches will not insist on polity or even doctrinal affinity for their expression. They will primarily serve to demonstrate the body of Christ locally through targeted efforts (like city-serve campaigns or massive worship gatherings). Missional communities are a manifestation of the network church at the micro level.

- Stand-alone missional communities will increase. Many post-congregational followers of Jesus will create missional communities that are not connected to any specific congregation. As house church practitioners have done, they will create networks and geographic associations for the purpose of fellowship, community service, and celebration.

- Church-planting strategies increasingly will adopt missional church applications for planting "the" church, rather than planting "a" church. Again, this approach will use a network architecture.

- Community development initiatives will create a hotbed of experimentation with missional communities. With the rise of altruism in America, more and more people are finding ways to tackle big issues that confront our communities. Jesus followers will get more sophisticated at being able to introduce intentional spiritual conversations with these community volunteers. Missional communities will emerge out of this cultural mix as people with similar passions and interests find other ways to connect with each other.

- Boomers will feed the missional communities movement. Known for their need to reinvent everything, Boomers are and will be at the forefront of this development. Empty-nesting Boomers are especially bored with and burned out by the program church. They are also intrigued by the idea of using their talent and treasure to make a difference in the community where they live. Missional communities allow this generational cohort a distinctive way forward, a way to script another chapter in their relentless pursuit of reengineering, reimagining, reinventing, repositioning, renewing—all things *re* are Boomer territory.

Some Issues Will Need to Be Explored Further in the Days Ahead

We are on the very front end of the missional communities' developmental curve. Much of what will come has not yet been imagined. However, the following issues are sure to capture some attention and will need to be addressed.

- Clergy will need to recognize that they need to give up control if they want to remain as players in missional communities. Missional communities are going to emerge anyway, so just what part clergy will play remains to be decided. A lot of that will depend on clergy's reaction to this new movement—and many are threatened by a church life form that doesn't center on them. Missional communities still allow plenty of room for teaching, coaching, missional strategizing, spiritual formation—roles that clergy can play. However, the church as congregation has produced a high-control need among many of its leaders that might make it difficult for them to respond positively to this new outbreak of Spirit initiatives unless they are willing to reconfigure their roles.

- Funding mechanisms are going to have to be developed. Actually, the funding of the missional community itself will not be the issue. These life forms require very little funding to sustain. The issue is what is going to happen to the money that is currently being funneled through the congregation. If missional communities are connected with congregations then I suspect their offerings will be, too; however, I also suspect there will not be as much central control. People increasingly enjoy deploying their resources directly to the projects and missions that capture their passions and dreams. Congregations, however, need to realize they can provide a great service to missional communities in this regard. They can hook them up with other resources, give them a charitable gift credit for tax purposes, and offer their relational capital in a community. All of this is a service that can and should be monetized. Simply put, they can charge missional communities for these services.

- Theology will be rewritten with a less congregation-centric bias. Most of the writings on the nature of the church and its practices reflect and assume the predominant model of church as congregation. Current and future efforts of missional thinkers will be directed at creating theology that is more street level, kingdom-centric. For instance, how is the fivefold ministry distributed in a network church? Or, how does the apostolic gifting show up in domains other than church? Business, education, sports—these and other domains have apostolic leaders in them, but in a congregation-centric paradigm this gift has been limited to congregational expression and application. Times of cultural upheaval have always produced new theological constructs. Augustine was writing as the Roman Empire was collapsing. The Reformation thinkers generated their systems as the medieval world was giving way to the modern era. A new world requires a new theological contextualization.

Getting Started

Perhaps you are reading this and are itching to get going. You are sold on experimenting with this new life form. Where do you begin? Here are a few ideas:

- The most promising option is in some small-group context. If you are a church leader with responsibilities for small-group oversight (yours or maybe the entire congregation's small-group program), you can remake the small-group experience to become more like a missional community. One small-group pastor called all the church small-group leaders together and fired them! Then he immediately hired them back as missional community leaders. If you are in a small group, but not the leader, you can lobby for your group to become more missionally intentional. Core aspects of missional communities that can be a part of any small-group experience include some external focus of ministry or service combined with greater intentionality in helping members live more missionally in their everyday life (and be willing to be accountable for doing so!).

- A second possibility for launching missional communities lies with the individual or individuals who evidence some measure of spiritual entrepreneurship. These people might not have existing church responsibilities; in fact, they may have avoided church assignments, preferring instead to focus their spiritual energies outside the congregation. Or they may be leaders who have been successful at launching new church ministries in the past. Now is the time to engage these people in a new spiritual venture. As entrepreneurs they are more open to the risks involved and are more comfortable with figuring things out in the process of creating something new.

- A third option for developing missional communities is to build off the passions that people have for helping the community in various ways. Some people really have a drive to help kids learn. Others are drawn to ministries of mercy for those who are profoundly needy at the margins of society. Still others find energy in taking up causes of social injustice or special needs groups. Missional communities can be formed around these pursuits by helping people be spiritually intentional in how they involve others to join them in their efforts. This starting point may actually prove to be the most natural way of engaging people who are not a part of any church as congregation, yet have spiritual interests and a desire to help others.

- A fourth idea for launching missional communities is . . . your idea! While you have been reading this book you might have had some great ideas of what kind of missional community you would like to be a part of. If you have gleaned anything from our discussion, surely it is that there is lots of room for experimentation. Mix and match elements you have found that captured you in the stories you have read—or try something else. Your imagination has been stimulated and you dream of what could be. *Go for it!*

Orchestral concert-goers are acquainted with the dissonant and chaotic sounds emanating from the orchestra pit prior to the performance. Musicians create a cacophony of noise as they tune their instruments and warm up for the show. No one thinks the lack of harmony or coordination is a sign of trouble. In fact, just the opposite is true. This is necessary preparation for the performance. The unconnected riffs actually increase the anticipation for what is to come. The seeming pandemonium gives way to organized beauty once the conductor takes the stand.

We are warming up for the next great performance of the church. It is a collaborative score called "The Church as Missional Communities." Some people are already in the pit, making noise. Others are being recruited. This is your chance. Now is the time. Grab your instrument. The Conductor is approaching the podium.

The world waits for the music.

About the Author

Dr. Reggie McNeal enjoys helping people, leaders, and Christian organizations pursue more intentional lives. He currently serves as the missional leadership specialist for Leadership Network of Dallas, Texas.

Reggie's past experience involves over a decade as a denominational executive and leadership development coach. He also served in local congregational leadership for over twenty years, including being the founding pastor of a new church. Reggie has lectured or taught as adjunct faculty for multiple seminaries, including Fuller Theological (Pasadena, California), Southwestern Baptist (Ft. Worth, Texas), Golden Gate Baptist (San Francisco, California), Trinity Divinity School (Deerfield, Illinois), Columbia International (Columbia, South Carolina), and Seminary of the Southwest (Austin, Texas). In addition, he has served as a consultant to local church, denomination, and para-church leadership teams, as well as seminar developer and presenter for thousands of church leaders across North America. He has also been a resource for the United States Army Office of the Chief of Chaplains (the Pentagon), the United States Army Chaplain School (Ft. Jackson, South Carolina), air force chaplains, and the Air Education and Training Command. Reggie's work also extends to the business sector, including the Gallup Organization.

Reggie has contributed to numerous publications and church leadership journals. His books include *Revolution in Leadership* (Abingdon Press, 1998), *A Work of Heart: Understanding How God Shapes Spiritual Leaders* (Jossey-Bass, 2000), *The Present Future* (Jossey-Bass, 2003), *Practicing Greatness* (Jossey-Bass, 2006), *Get a Life!* (B&H Publishing, 2007), *Missional Renaissance: Changing the Scorecard for the Church* (Jossey-Bass, 2009).

Reggie's education includes a B.A. degree from the University of South Carolina and the M.Div. and Ph.D. degrees, both from Southwestern Baptist Theological Seminary. Reggie and his wife, Cathy, make their home in Columbia, South Carolina.

INDEX

The Present Future

Six Tough Questions for the Church

Reggie McNeal

Paper
ISBN: 978-0-470-4315-5

"This is the most courageous book I have ever read on church life. McNeal nails the problem on the head. Be prepared to be turned upside down and shaken loose of all your old notions of what church is and should be in today's world."

—**George Cladis**, author, *Leading the Team-Based Church*

In *The Present Future*, author, consultant, and church leadership developer Reggie McNeal debunks old assumptions about church leadership and provides an overall strategy to help church leaders move forward in an entirely different and much more effective way.

In this provocative book, McNeal identifies the six most important realities that church leaders must address including: recapturing the spirit of Christianity and replacing "church growth" with a wider vision of kingdom growth; developing disciples instead of church members; fostering the rise of a new apostolic leadership; focusing on spiritual formation rather than church programs; and shifting from prediction and planning to preparation for the challenges of an uncertain world. McNeal contends that by changing the questions church leaders ask themselves about their congregations and their plans, they can frame the core issues and approach the future with new eyes, new purpose, and new ideas.

Written for congregational leaders, pastors, and staff leaders, **The Present Future** captures the urgency of a future that is literally now upon us, in a thoughtful, vigorous way. It is filled with examples of leaders and churches who are emerging into a new identity and purpose, and rediscovering the focus of their mission within new spiritual dimensions.

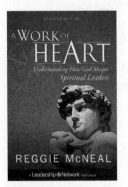

A Work of Heart
Understanding How God Shapes Spiritual Leaders
Updated Edition

Reggie McNeal

Cloth
ISBN: 978-1-118-10318-0

"It is not just the skills of ministry that are important. The heart-sculpting work of God creates quality ministries. *A Work of Heart* explains how God is shaping each of us for future service."
— **Bob Buford**, founding chairman, Leadership Network

Revised and updated edition of the classic work on spiritual leadership

In **A Work of Heart**, bestselling author and missional expert Reggie McNeal helps leaders reflect on the ways in which God is shaping them by letting us see God at work in the lives of four quintessential biblical leaders: Moses, David, Jesus, and Paul. McNeal identifies the formative influences upon these leaders, which he sees as God's ways of working in their lives: the same influences at work today forming leaders for ministry in our times. He explores the shaping influence of culture, call, community, conflict, and the commonplace.

Using illustrative stories of contemporary leaders opening their hearts to God's guidance, McNeal show how—just as God used these influences to shape biblical leaders—God is using the same influences to shape the hearts of Christian leaders today.

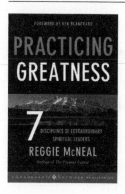

Practicing Greatness

7 Disciplines of Extraordinary Spiritual Leaders

Reggie McNeal

Foreword by Ken Blanchard

Cloth

ISBN: 978-0-7879-7753-5

"The depth and breadth of wisdom in this book is just short of unbelievable. Good leaders aspiring to be great leaders will do well to read this book and allow it to probe and shape their lives."
—**Bill Easum**, Easum, Bandy & Associates

How do good spiritual leaders become great leaders?

Based on his experience coaching and mentoring thousands of Christian leaders across a broad spectrum of ministry settings, bestselling leadership expert and consultant Reggie McNeal helps spiritual leaders understand that they will self-select into or out of greatness.

In this important book, McNeal shows how great spiritual leaders are committed consciously and intentionally to seven spiritual disciplines, habits of heart and mind that shape both their character and competence: self-awareness, self-management, a lifelong commitment to self-development through personal growth and learning, a sense of mission, learning to make great decisions, the commitment to live in community, and the intentional practice of solitude and contemplation.

Practicing Greatness goes beyond mere clichés and inspirational thoughts to be a hard-hitting resource for leaders who aspire to go from being just good enough to being a great leader who blesses others.

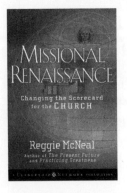

Missional Renaissance
Changing the Scorecard for the Church

Reggie McNeal

Cloth
ISBN: 978-0-470-24344-2

"Any new book by Reggie McNeal is something of an event, and this book is no exception. Not only is this an excellent introduction to missional Christianity, but it establishes a much-needed metric by which we can assess the vitality of this highly significant new movement."
—**Alan Hirsch**, author, *The Forgotten Ways, Rejesus,* and *The Shaping of Things to Come*; founding director, Forge Mission Training System; co-founder, shapevine.com

Missional Renaissance is McNeal's much-anticipated follow-up to his groundbreaking, best-selling book, *The Present Future*, which quickly became one of the definitive works on the "missional church movement."

In *Missional Renaissance*, Reggie McNeal shows the three significant shifts in church leaders' thinking and behavior that will allow their congregations to chart a course toward becoming truly a missional congregation. To embrace the missional model, church leaders and members must shift from an internal to an external focus, ending the church as exclusive social club model; from running programs and ministries to developing people as its core activity; and from church-based leadership to community-engaged leadership.

The book is filled with in-depth discussions of what it means to become a missional congregation and important information on how to make the transition. *Missional Renaissance* offers a clear path for any leader or congregation that wans to breathe new life into the church and to become revitalized as true followers of Jesus.

The Present Future DVD Collection

Six Tough Questions for the Church, Set

Reggie McNeal

ISBN: 978-0-7879-8637-5

"Reggie McNeal throws a lifeline to church leaders who are struggling with consumer-oriented congregations wanting church for themselves. The *Present Future* will recharge your passion."

—**Rev. Robert R. Cushman**, senior pastor,
Princeton Alliance Church, Plainsboro, NJ

Despite the many good things we can point to, the many faithful folks who are doing their best, all is not well with the Christian church in America. What's missing, as Reggie McNeal points out in his DVD presentation of **The Present Future: Six Tough Questions for the Church**, is the gritty realization that the way we are doing church is just plain wrong. And worse than wrong, it jeopardizes the church's mission. In this set of DVDs, Reggie McNeal reframes the issues facing the church, replacing wrong key questions with tough questions that must be asked.

Filmed live before a studio audience, in this DVD set Reggie McNeal teaches participants how to recognize the six most important new realities that church leaders must face if they are to move beyond "churchianity" to a more authentic and missional Christian faith. By changing the questions church leaders ask themselves about their congregations and their mission, they can reshape the Christian movement in North America.

The package includes:

- 1 Leader's Guide
- 1 Participant's Guide
- 4 DVDs

Additional Participant's Guides may also be purchased separately,

ISBN: 978-0-7879-9170-8

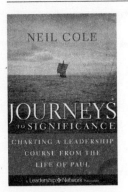

Journeys to Significance

Charting a Leadership Course from the Life of Paul

Neil Cole

Hardcover
ISBN: 978-1-118-00544-6

"This interpretive biography of Paul is a valuable resource for a leader who wants to pursue the *Leadership Mandate* (Hebrews 13:7-8) and learn from Paul's examples."

— **Dr. J. Robert Clinton**, Professor of Leadership, School of Intercultural Studies, Fuller Theological Seminary

"The life and ministry of the apostle Paul prove a treasure trove for leaders' development when masterfully explored by Neil Cole. No matter what life/ministry phase you are in, you will find insights that help you better understand how you are being shaped for your leadership assignment."

— **Reggie McNeal**, author of *Missional Renaissance*, *The Present Future*, and *A Work of Heart*

In *Journeys to Significance*, bestselling author and organic church leader Neil Cole takes us on a journey as we follow the life of the apostle Paul and learn valuable lessons about how God forms a leader over the course of his or her life. It's not about just reaching the end—it's about finishing well and keeping your eye on the ultimate goal, not on short-term wins or losses. *Journeys to Significance* provides valuable insights to help any leader (or aspiring leader) to build upon each journey so that finishing strong is not only possible, but is a clear and practical focus in the here and now.

NEIL COLE is an experienced and innovative church planter and pastor. He is the founder of the Awakening Chapels, which are reaching young postmodern people in urban settings, and a founder and executive director of Church Multiplication Associates. He is the author of several books including *Organic Church* and *Church 3.0*, both from Jossey-Bass.